I0667890

THE STRUGGLE IS ONE

Base 504793 (546709) 11-81

## Brazil

International boundary
Estado or território boundary
National capital
Estado or território capital
Railroad
Paved road
Unpaved road

0        500 Kilometers
0        500 Miles

The islands of Fernando de Noronha, Rocas, Trindade, Martin Vaz, and Penedos de São Pedro e São Paulo are not shown.

Trindade and Martin Vaz are under the jurisdiction of Espirito Santo. Fernando de Noronha has território status.

Boundary representation is not necessarily authoritative.

# THE STRUGGLE IS ONE

## VOICES AND VISIONS
## OF LIBERATION

MEV PULEO

STATE UNIVERSITY OF NEW YORK PRESS

Cover photo: On the feast of Corpus Cristi, bishops, priests, nuns and lay people march in the streets of São Paulo under a banner supporting labor unions, "A worker outside of a union is like a needle in a haystack". Bishop Angélico, who in 1990 was replaced by the more traditional Bishop Legal, marches in the front row of the clergy (the robed man to the left). June 21, 1987.

Published by
State University of New York Press, Albany

© 1994 State University of New York

All rights reserved

Printed in the United States of America

No part of this book may be used or reproduced
in any manner whatsoever without written permission
except in the case of brief quotations embodied in
critical articles and reviews.

For information, address State University of New York
Press, State University Plaza, Albany, N.Y., 12246

Production by Diane Ganeles
Marketing by Theresa Abad Swierzowski

Library of Congress Cataloging-in-Publication Data

Puleo, Mev, 1963–
   The struggle is one : voices and visions of liberation / Mev
Puleo.
      p.    cm.
   Includes bibliographical references and index.
   ISBN 0-7914-2013-2 (cloth : alk. paper). — ISBN 0-7914-2014-0
(pbk. : alk. paper)
   1. Catholic Church—Brazil—History—20th century.  2. Liberation
theology.  3. Catholics—Brazil—Interviews.  4. Church and social
problems—Brazil.  5. Church and social problems—Catholic Church.
6. Brazil—Church history—20th century.  7. Brazil—Social
conditions—1964–  I. Title.
BX1466.2.P85   1994
282'.81'09045—dc20                                    93-37873
                                                          CIP

10 9 8 7 6 5 4 3

In honor of my friends
Goreth
and
Toinha
their children
and future grandchildren.

# CONTENTS

# FOREWORD

## ROBERT MCAFEE BROWN

If I were to choose a single book by means of which to introduce North Americans to the real meaning of liberation theology, it would be this book. For liberation theology is not about dogmas or documents or church councils or even social analysis, nearly so much as it is about *people*, God's people, and that embraces all. Neglect that starting point and all else will be misunderstood, a cardboard replica lacking three dimensions. The worst thing we can do is to reduce liberation theology to another theological fad, riding the crest of the wave for the moment, but soon to be displaced by the next new set of speculations.

This does not for a moment reduce liberation theology to a "soft" discipline, about which it is appropriate to have feelings, but about which one had better not think too much. Every part of it is exacting—just like the environs of the poor from which it comes. Every part of it takes account of what came before—not necessarily for uncritical incorporation but for reflective thought and probable redefinition. Every part of it breathes a context—the lives and deaths of the oppressed peoples of the earth. Every part of it breathes hope—for out of environments and thoughts and contexts new things can come, and do.

But the best vehicle of its transmission is not the printed page or even the spoken word, but the committed lives of its adherents. And here is where Mev Puleo's *The Struggle is One: Voices and Visions of Liberation* breaks new ground, for its pages show us photographs of those who speak and live and die, and the contexts where they work and worship. No longer do we confront merely speculation or theory, but people, once again "God's own people," authentic beyond any measurement of it since their words and lives are *one*.

Liberation theology needs its books and systems and theologians and structures, but most of all it needs its witnesses—people for the most part without graduate degrees or tenured chairs or international acclaim—those who not only live out their faith but (as a second definition of "witness" reminds us) are willing if necessary to die for it. Every person in this book has faced that possibility.

Do not only read their words. Gaze at their faces also. For finally we cannot understand one without the other.

A homeless man sleeps on the steps of the Catholic cathedral in downtown São Paulo. Street children often sleep on these steps, as they feel safer from death squads when they are near a church.

# Acknowledgments

First, acknowledgment goes to the Jonathan M. Daniels Memorial Fellowship, which enabled me to travel to Brazil, seeking to bridge worlds. Jonathan M. Daniels, an Episcopal Divinity Student, was shot and killed in 1965 while working for civil rights in Alabama.

Special thanks go to the gracious Brazilian hosts who welcomed and assisted me: Bishop Luís Fernandez; the Benedictine Sisters in Recife; the Irish sisters in João Pessoa; Tereza Cavalcanti and her family; the generous Maryknoll Missionary team—especially Dan McLaughlin and Anne Archbold; and the remarkable Lilia Azevedo and João Xerri, O.P., true exemplars of solidarity.

A warm and grateful thank you to all of my stateside "base communities" for their support and encouragement: the Cambridge Sunday Night Group (especially Mary Claire Ryan, S.H.C.J., Susan Koehler, and Kevin Schneider, S.J.); the Berkeley Christian Solidarity Project; Oakland Pax Christi; the Wednesday Morning Meditation Group and BASE (Brasil Action and Solidarity Exchange). I also give thanks to Robert Ellsberg, who challenged me to pursue this project; to Meg Guider, O.S.F., Rich Wood, Libby Wood, Sam Bowles and Dana Bell who helped me clarify my vision; to Tom Ferentz, for darkroom assistance; to Laura Krueger and Sheri Hostetler for their invaluable editing skills; and to SUNY Press editor Lois Patton—without her spark of interest this work may never have come to fruition.

I also thank my parents, Peter and Evelyn Puleo, who first brought me to Brazil in 1977, who helped open my eyes to both the suffering and the beauty in our world, and who continue to support me even when my vocation takes me far from home. And, finally, my heart goes out in gratitude to Mark Chmiel, my travel companion, colleague and husband, whose encouragement sustains me. You have reminded me that this book is an act of faith.

# INTRODUCTION

*Solid and majestic. The stone-carved Jesus towers over the ten million inhabitants of Rio de Janeiro.*

*Animated and pleading. The eyes of children peer into the windows of our tour bus as it snakes up the hill towards the famous statue of "Christ the Redeemer."*

*Through the bus windows on the left we see posh hotels, immaculate beaches and expensive tourist shops. The windows on the right tell a different story, of ramshackle homes, children in rags, young and old begging for our coins. The Christ statue comes in and out of view as I gape to the left and to the right.*

I was fourteen years old, touring Rio de Janeiro with my family, when I first rode that bus to the statue on the hill. That day, as images of opulence and misery rocked my world, a crisis of conscience took root in me.

The questions planted that day took years to find words: What does it mean to be a "Christian"—a follower of the way of Jesus—in a world of contradictions and conflicts? What does it mean to be on the way to Jesus when I view worlds of poverty from an air-conditioned tour bus? The early Christians were called "followers of the way." What way must we, who live inspired by Jesus of Nazareth, follow today?

Little did I know sixteen years ago that my wrestling with these questions would lead me back to Brazil. Yet, in this Brazil of contrasts and conflicts, I have discovered remarkable people who have walked this hill before me.

Followers of the way, they have tried to speak and move across the monstrous gap between the privileged and the poor. Bishops who walk the way of voluntary poverty and risk death denouncing injustice, defending the poor. Theologians who allow

1

the reality of other people's suffering to turn their theories up-side down. Peasants and nearly illiterate shantytown-dwellers who opt to lead communities of faith and resistance. Middle-class married persons and members of religious communities who sacrifice lives of comfort to be available to those in need.

֎ ֎ ֎

And what of this Brazil, host of Christ the Redeemer atop the hillside marked by opulence and marred by misery? What of this place that has given birth to so many followers of the way?

Brazil—a country rich in minerals, rainforest, farm land and a diversity of peoples and cultures. Brazil—a country scarred by inequality, injustice and premature death. Eighty-seven percent of the arable land lies idle in the hands of wealthy speculators, the Amazon rainforest is being toppled by an onslaught of cattle-ranchers, two-thirds of the people are malnourished, and seven million children live on the streets.

Yet in this suffering, strife-torn land, a new way of being church has come to life. Three people walking on the beach one day—a theologian, a writer and a bishop—christened this new experience "ecclesiogenesis." *the birth of a church.*

For in this Brazil we find tens of thousands of base ecclesial communities (*comunidades eclesiais de base*—known in Brazil as "CEBs"), where women and men reflect on the Word of God, which empowers them in their struggle to make the Reign of God a reality here and now. Here we find scores of prolific, committed liberation theologians reflecting on questions of faith starting from the reality of their people who are impoverished and op-pressed. Here we find the National Brazilian Bishops Conference (known as the "CNBB"), second in size only to that of the U.S. For twenty years the CNBB has issued documents defending the peo-ple's rights to land, food and political participation.

Most strikingly, this is a church that has experienced pro-found conversion, a church whose authenticity is proved by the blood of its many martyrs.

Brazil's military takeover in 1964 inspired nuns and priests to take to the streets, praying the rosary in gratitude and carry-ing banners that said, "The Church thanks God that the military saved us from communism!" Within a few years, however, the severity of government-sponsored repression provoked an outcry from the church hierarchy.

Not unlike other military dictatorships in South America in the 1960s and 70s, Brazil's military government carried out the torture, 'disappearances' and summary executions of thousands of dissidents and grassroots activists during these decades. Church workers and community animators (lay ministers who organize grassroots communities) appeared on death lists because of their work with students, farmers, Indians and workers. The blood of nuns, priests and lay catechists soon mingled with that of lawyers, unionists, students and peasants committed to the struggle for justice.[†]

For the next twenty years under military rule, the Catholic church provided the country's only relatively safe space for community organizing, since labor, student and political movements were outlawed or crushed. Championing the cause of human rights, the church took up the prophetic tasks of denouncing the injustice and abuses, and announcing the Reign of God—not an otherworldly kingdom, but a Reign that takes root in the soil of human community, equality and dignity.

This was an era of conversion and commitment for the whole of Latin America. During the 1968 Latin American Episcopal Conference (*Conferencia General del Espiscopado Latinoamericano*, generally known as "CELAM") in Medellín, Colombia, the continent's Catholic bishops made the historic declaration of a preferential option for the poor. This option, theologically based on a belief in the God of life who draws close to those in the grip of death, was reaffirmed at the 1979 CELAM gathering in Puebla, Mexico, and has been echoed since then by the World Council of Churches and many other religious bodies and congregations. In 1971, Peru's mestizo pastor and theologian, Gustavo Gutiérrez, published the ground-breaking *A Theology of Liberation*, which was followed by hundreds of theological and pastoral works from the liberationist perspective, many from Brazilians, both Catholic and Protestant.

This line of pastoral practice and academic reflection has disrupted the status quo of both church and state. While Pope John Paul II has affirmed the preferential option for the poor (which he also calls the preferential "love" for the poor), the Vatican's Congregation for the Doctrine of the Faith (CDF), headed by Cardinal Joseph Ratzinger, has issued two instructions warning of

---

†The book *Torture in Brazil: A Report by the Archdiocese of São Paulo* (New York: Vintage Books, 1986) documents torture during the period of military dictatorship in Brazil. This work is a result of a courageous crusade led by Paulo Evaristo Arns, Catholic Cardinal of São Paulo, and Presbyterian minister Jaime Wright, who organized the clandestine photocopying of thousands of legal and military files.

certain dangers in liberation theology (1984, 1986). Moreover, the Vatican has given warnings to more than a dozen Latin American theologians and bishops and has criticized the CEBs for subverting the proper authority structure of the church. The CDF also silenced Brazilian theologian Leonardo Boff from May 9, 1985, until March 29, 1986, in reaction to his provocative critique of Vatican power, *Church: Charism and Power*. After seven more years of relentless harassment and censorship, Boff, finally left the Franciscan priesthood, but not the church, to teach and write without constraint.

The Vatican trend of suspicion, criticism and censure continues in the appointments of conservative bishops throughout Latin America; the 1989 closing of a seminary that was committed to the option for the poor in Recife, Brazil; the 1989 division of the archdiocese of São Paulo, a severe blow to the advanced network of CEBs; the censoring of the "Word-Life" project which was publishing interpretations of the Bible informed by poor communities; and repeated interventions to both censor and control the Latin American Conference of Religious (CLAR).

Secular forces have also opposed the Latin American church of liberation. A 1969 report prepared by Nelson Rockefeller urged the Nixon administration to monitor the developments in the Latin American Church. The Santa Fe documents (1980, 1989), prepared for the Reagan and Bush administrations by the Council for Inter-American Security, warned that liberation theology is rife with dangerous political doctrines. A 1986 report by the Brazilian National Security Council described the progressive church as an "enemy" and denounced the CNBB as a "serious threat to democracy." In 1987 the heads of fifteen Latin American armies, including military representatives from the U.S., attacked liberation theology, denouncing several theologians by name.

In what makes for a deplorable case of strange bedfellows, many of the people under Vatican scrutiny, such as Bishop Pedro Casaldáliga, have also been targeted by local elites and their hired thugs. The Vatican chastised and nearly silenced Casaldáliga for his visits to Nicaragua and his failure to go to Rome for his *ad limina* visit, the periodic visit to Rome required of all bishops. Meanwhile, because of Casaldáliga's support for land reform and his outspoken defense of the rights of the poor, local landowners threatened him with death and assassinated his close friend, Father João Bosco. Even after Brazil's transition to a civilian government in 1985, the new constitution of 1988, and direct elections in 1989, the blood of the martyrs—lay pastoral ministers, priests and believers—still flows in the cities and countryside of Brazil.

ᔥᐧ ᔥᐧ ᔥᐧ

Through images, narratives and interviews, this book seeks to give a face and a voice to this new way of being church, to the silenced and the outspoken, to the privileged and the impoverished.

Across Brazil, these people have made an option for God and an option for the poor, which, for them, is one and the same: following the God of life who draws closest to those in the clutches of death.

In Portuguese, *a luta*, or in Spanish, *la lucha*, is the struggle for survival, the struggle to bring about the Reign of God: a piece of bread, a plot of land, a just wage, a day-care center. These are not given from above but won from below.

These struggles are not won alone, but in communion with God and in community with one another. In their struggle for life the people of God are one—peasants, poets, professors, bishops, great-grandmothers. One in their passion for God, one in their risking of death for the cause of justice. One with us as we take up the same struggle for life, against death in all its forms. For this book also seeks to be a bridge between peoples North and South, companions in the struggle, fellow followers of the way.

The struggle is both individual and social. For many in the First World, death may wear the mask of alcoholism, cut-throat competition or an inner emptiness in the midst of material abundance. Here, life may be fostered by support groups, solitude and simpler lifestyles. Yet these individual afflictions are reinforced by social structures, the same structures that oppress the poor.

For the growing number of disenfranchised in the North and the masses of marginalized abroad, death comes in the form of hunger, joblessness, systemic oppression. Here, life is won in the victories of community organizing, political pressure, strikes and demonstrations. Yet the exploited poor and social activists also have hungers of the heart—hungers for intimacy, meaning and consolation when social projects fail.

For holistic liberation, the struggle must reach both the individual and the societal, it must embrace the personal and the political. As Bible scholar Carlos Mesters says, "We may start at different points, but we arrive together. The struggle is one struggle."

Whether we are struggling to recover from our addictions or struggling for the right to farm the land, the struggle is one. The struggle against racism reaches from the streets of Washington, D.C. to the slums of Rio. The struggle for decent housing is fought from St. Louis to São Paulo. The struggle to be free from anxiety and depression, the struggle to love and serve, bridges all peoples, places and ages.

We may start at different points, but we arrive together. And we are sure to arrive sooner if we walk in solidarity—rich and poor, woman and man, indigenous and white and black, Brazilian and North American.

This book gives voice to the struggle and puts a face on those who struggle.

Here we will meet the world famous and the often anonymous midwives of change. Here we will meet the *persons* behind the personalities—the pilgrims, pioneers and prophets of our day.

Here we will meet poets and mystics who know that God is dreaming with the community for a new world of justice and joy.

Here we will meet the martyrs and saints who, like the prophet Ezekiel, are blowing the spirit of hope and life into the brittle bones of suffering and death.

Hear, then, their voices and their visions.

Hear their journeys, their turning points, their choices. Hear their insights and understandings. Hear their interpretations of church conflicts. Hear their hopes for the future of liberation theology, for women in the church, for the birth of an ecologically-grounded spirituality.

Hear from the poor their word for the rich.

Hear from the privileged, who have opted for the poor, their message for those who wish to make that same choice.

Hear the personal invitation to solidarity from your sisters and brothers South of the border. Hear the prayers and desires of this hopeful, struggling people.

Hear in their words the echo of your own struggles and desires. And see in their faces a reflection of your own.

ॐ ॐ ॐ

The following chapters are composed of photographs and interviews with base community members, lay pastoral ministers, theologians and Catholic bishops. Each chapter opens with photographic images of the person interviewed and, in most cases, images of their home, work site, city or region.

The interview begins in storytelling style—each section a vignette of the person's background, conversion, spirituality, struggles and dreams. This narrative is followed by questions and answers on subjects such as the future of liberation theology and the CEBs, internal church conflicts, the option for the poor and the environment. Each interview closes with a personal message to the reader, a concrete suggestion for solidarity.

All of the interviews were conducted in Portuguese and each person generously granted me full permission to translate, edit and employ a creative style of presentation. It is difficult to convey the lyrical quality of the human voice, the ebb and flow of conversation. People don't speak in paragraphs or outlines! I have tried to present the material in a way that is faithful to the spirit of each person. I hope the photographic images add texture to the voices.

The interviews also vary greatly in length, the portraits in quantity. I met some people, like Ivone Gebara and Frei Betto, for a mere forty-five minutes in the midst of their busy days, so our photos and words were rushed; I spent two days with Dom Pedro and nearly a week with Goreth and Toinha, gathering many images and enjoying longer conversations. This explains any unevenness in presentation.

Finally, I labored long over the order in which to present this material—do I start with the famous or the anonymous? While readers are encouraged to skip around the book according to their own interests and inspiration, I have opted to begin with the people at the base. Borrowing an image the Boff brothers use to describe the three levels of liberation theology, the people are the unseen roots (*popular* level) that anchor the more visible trunk (the *pastoral* level of bishops and pastoral agents) and the very visible branches (the *professional* level of theologians). Hence the Vatican can lop off a branch by silencing a theologian, but the roots hold the tree in place and ensure it will grow again.

ॐ ॐ ॐ

Yes, the way up the hill to Christ the Redeemer is a bumpy, sometimes dangerous ride. And I have come to believe that we, the privileged, are invited to get off the bus and plant our feet squarely beside the journeying people, walking with the God who is present in those on *both* sides of the road. We may all start at different places but, as people seeking to follow the way of liberation and justice, we will arrive together as we learn to walk with one another. One, in the struggle.

# 1

## Maria da Silva Miguel

I am woman-mother and warrior,
the stove is no longer my limit.
I am called queen of the home,
but I am greater than ocean and sea.
I am mother, I give life,
I am a woman, pain.
I am a warrior, a bird—I sing!

—from "The People is Poet"

by Maria Miguel

*I interviewed Maria da Silva Miguel inside her home at the eastern periphery of São Paulo. Maria lives in a small, one room concrete structure in a hillside favela.† A large wooden cross adorns the wall of her single room home. Her dresser is arranged like an altar, the Bible resting prominently at the center under a protective plastic cover.*

---

†*Favelas*, usually described as "shantytowns," are squatter villages where people originally build homes out of any scrap materials they can find. Many people try to gradually improve their homes, adding firm walls and concrete floors, hoping to eventually obtain a legal title to the land they occupy.

Maria Miguel sits with her two great-grandchildren on the steps outside of her house.

*Maria Miguel is a great-grandmother to six young children, two of whom live with her. She started writing poetry when she was sixty-five, and now writes songs for her church and for political demonstrations. A national Brazilian religious magazine recently published one of her songs of struggle, "The People is Poet." Maria is active in the land movement, the health movement, the local Bible study group and is passionately involved in local women's groups.*

*Born of slaves, Maria is deeply concerned about the continuing oppression of blacks in Brazil. Roughly fifty percent of Brazil's population is black, most of them descendents of slaves. Brazil officially abolished slavery in 1888.*

*Periodically during the interview, Maria Miguel rocks with laughter—"I really like to write about women—because I'm a woman!" In her poetry she calls herself a "warrior." That she is, a warrior and a rock, and a reed for God's voice, giving voice to the people.*

*After the interview she offers Anne, my lay missioner friend, and me coffee, apologizing that she doesn't have any bread. I leave her simple home warmed by her welcome, humbled and inspired by her songs.*

ᔮ ᔮ ᔮ

I was born in a little rural town in the state of Minas Gerais [central Brazil]. When I was fifteen, I moved from the countryside to the big city. I arrived in São Paulo on the third day of Carnival—and I thought they were giving me a big party!

I went to work as a maid, and my first child was born in the house of the people I worked for, and my second child died.

That's when my suffering began.

My suffering continued throughout my life. I was so poor. I worked to make Brazil a great country, and I didn't achieve anything.

My only achievement is the life God has given me. For me, this is a marvelous thing! God has given me *life*—this is everything. Thanks be to God.

I praise God all the time!

ᔮ ᔮ ᔮ

Altar in room of Maria da Silva Miguel.

A favela in the Eastern Zone of São Paulo, much
like the one surrounding Maria Miguel's home.

My mother lived near the time of slavery.

Although I think the times of slavery were awful, I think it's worse now. You see, where I was raised there was always at least a cup of milk on the table or a chicken in the yard.

My mother came to visit me in São Paulo and was so upset when she saw our lives. She said, "I already lived in slavery, but the slavery you are living here is much worse. Here in São Paulo you have to run away from men in the street. In my day if we saw a man in the street we ran to catch up with him so we that had company and protection."

She also said that at least in slavery, people managed to eat. Sometimes the owners would half-bury the slave and whip them. The person would die or live, but the master never stopped feeding someone. Today, we are not whipped or half-buried, but we have no food to eat!

Thank God that I haven't starved yet. But, I lived through much hunger as a child.

Things are worse today. They really are.

The poor people of Brazil are really at "zero." The poor lack everything—a house, food, work. It's no good to be healthy if you have to live under a bridge!

From the time a child is born, it has problems—poor nutrition, lack of education. Most mothers also work as domestic maids, leaving the house early to help meet the "cost of life" since the husband doesn't earn enough.

The problem in Brazil is terrible—everyone has to work.

There are days when my grandchild asks me for an orange, and I don't have one to give. In some houses a child will ask for bread, and there is none. What a way for a child to grow up!

And the rich collaborate with this suffering. Yes, the powerful people are responsible, the whole society is. We don't bring these problems on ourselves. A child is not *born* marginalized! They become marginalized *after* they are born by the daily hardships of their lives.

No one likes to live like this.

ళ ళ ళ

There's also plenty of racism in Brazil.

Black people aren't very well accepted for various work positions simply because of their skin color. It really bothers me that people speak against blacks so much.

You know, if a white person is running down the street, they think he's jogging. But, if a black person is jogging, they think he's running away from the police or something, because black people are considered pickpockets and thieves. People always come down on black people.

White people rob at will, but no one says anything because they're afraid of the whites! And the white people are the ones who are really afraid of us—because if the people were united, we would do away with this kind of injustice. So long as we're not united, we'll never have liberation.

My hope for the future is liberation.

Liberation—that we have houses for our children and grandchildren. I don't know if I'll reach this dream of a house and a just salary, of dignity and justice for the poor. I may not reach it, but I have grandchildren and great-grandchildren.

I have hope for the young.

঺ ঺ ঺

Since I was little, I was raised in the Church.

But the church was, well, a bit closed then. The Bible was only for the priest and the Mass was in Latin. Thank God it all changed!

I abandoned the church for a time. But as the saying goes, "Those who don't return from love, return from pain." I returned from pain . . . from pain. I felt very sick, totally diminished, absolutely useless. Then I said to myself, "I know I've neglected the church. I need to search out the way of God."

So, about ten years ago I met Sister Josefa, who opened the way.

I went to Mass and she started to talk to me about the struggle. I tried to help her out, so I became involved with the movement to start a day-care center. Before too long I was in the land movement, the health movement and the Bible study group!

Now I work a lot with the women's movement in our region. I work in all of the movements, but, really, the struggle is the struggle of women. Thank God that we have women who are aware.

In my poem, "The People is Poet," *woman warrior* refers to the struggle.

*I am a woman warrior—I'm going to the struggle!* I'm going to the struggle to get our rights! It's not a struggle with guns. Our weapon is our word. We have the right to speak!

The struggle is when I leave my house to go after what I need. If we don't struggle, we won't get anything—we'll remain prisoners, crushed under the heel of the powerful people. No one will come knocking on our door to give us housing, health care, education, food. Not the mayor, not the government. We have to demand our rights. We have to cry out—this is the struggle!

And if we don't have faith, we won't succeed.

Our Bible group tries to wake people up to their oppression.

Some people aren't involved in the church or the struggle because they don't have much faith. Without faith, they're terribly discouraged by their oppression. We all have to remember God and do what we can.

🙚 🙚 🙚

I didn't start writing poetry until I was sixty-five. One day I just felt like writing poetry! I really like to write about women—because I'm a woman! Oh how I love to write poetry!

The priest asks me, "Dona Maria, do you have a message today?" It can be Fathers' Day or Mothers' Day or any day. I have poetry for every day!

Poetry is part of the struggle!

Poetry is good for us, good for our *spirit* and our *body* also, because happiness always strengthens our lives. My many, many sorrows and problems go away.

We, the people, speak through our music.

When we march in the streets, people who can hardly read or write understand what we're saying in the songs! We aren't looking for trouble when we march, but we're willing to risk prison if that's what it comes down to.

The music and words are a *release*. They let us breathe freely and give vent to our struggles. It's our way to name reality, to expose reality.

You see, when we struggle, we must have an open spirit.

If you are only burdened by problems and sorrows, you'll be closed. You won't be able to join in the struggle. We have to get beyond this weariness, these sorrows.

Some days I, too, feel so weighed down by my daily life struggles. But, thank God I have enough energy to get beyond this!

ఖ ఖ ఖ

I never lack for much, nor do my neighbors or friends. We only have to ask God. We are nourished by the strength of God and the Holy Spirit walks with us.

Our faith is in *God*. Without God we can't journey onward.

I pray very much for my companions in the struggle. I have my Bible there by my bed. I read it every night. I pray before I eat my food, and ask God to bless the nourishment that I'm going to eat.

My prayers are like sermons! If I don't pray for everyone, I can't sleep. Sometimes I lie down so tired, saying, "today I can't pray." But I get up and pray!

My faith is great, thanks be to God.

The grace of God sustains me.

ఖ ఖ ఖ

*Besides the acts of violence against women that you witness, how else would you describe the situation of women in your neighborhood?*

Women here are very discriminated against. In everything. With machismo, it seems that men are always ahead of women, more valued. A woman works and produces the same as a man. In addition to working at the factory, she works at home. She's discriminated against by her boss and by her husband.

My neighbor was attacked in back of her own house. Poor thing, she works at night in a restaurant. It was the bus driver, who knew she came home at that time, hiding and waiting for her. Finally the husband heard her screams.

We're disgusted with this kind of thing—we can't go out in the streets anymore! I get, well, not despairing, because I have much faith in God. But the way things are, there's just too much violence.

Maria, sitting at her kitchen table, reads from her
poetry notebook.

We're struggling for the liberation of women. Someday we will arrive!

*Do you think the wealthy also need liberation?*

Some people have so much money that they don't know what to spend it on! Money causes so much violence, such as people kidnapping for money.

The rich can only gain from the liberation of the poor. We want the right of equality and dignity for *everyone*. You see, I don't want rich people's money! No! I'm not going to rob anyone! We want—well, as I write in a song, *We want them to stoop down and give us the crumbs from their tables.* Only this!

As it is, if the poor want to eat a piece of bread, they have to ask the rich. We want the rich to have compassion on the poor. We want at least their crumbs—but we want much more than this! We are the people of God, and we're not being treated like the people of God. God doesn't want this! Jesus wants us to practice faith and love and unity. *This* is what God wants for the people of God.

*There are many people around the world who would like to be more committed. What can we do to be on the side of the poor?*

I always ask God to open the hearts of these people—the middle-class and even the rich. They seem to have closed hearts. But, their hearts are of flesh just like ours! I'd like them to think a bit more about the poor. God always said, "Love one another as I've loved you." And God loves all of us.

God isn't responsible for the suffering here. People are responsible—the powerful, the rich people who want to be richer. They forget about the poor, who are becoming more and more poor.

So, I ask God to open their hearts. I ask God to make the powerful have *compassion* on the poor who work so hard for them, give them a just salary so the poor can live in dignity.

*What can we do to be more in solidarity with your people?*

People there should get to know the day-to-day lives of people here. This would give us more strength! I'd like people to know our suffering, so they could help us.

People here are very skeptical, they're losing all faith. You see, our President [Collar de Mello] said he would do away with poverty, but he really means he will do away with the poor! He isn't changing the unjust financial situation, he is killing the poor through hunger and homelessness.

We need people to raise awareness so we can get out of this abyss. We suffer so much, there are no words to express it! People are begging in the streets! We know there are countries that are better organized. I don't want wealth, but I don't want anyone to be poor. Please, help us do away with our misery.

We have hope that one day things will really change. If I don't see it, maybe my grandchildren will, or even my great-grandchildren.

# 2

# SALOMÉ COSTA

I think when you feel suffering in your own skin, you can either become discouraged and think everything's over, or you can become more animated in the common struggle for life.

When I was in the hospital with tuberculosis, I lost both of my parents . . . Then my two brothers also died. But when people ask, "Do you live alone in São Paulo?" I answer, "No, I have a very *big* family!" I really feel that we are sisters and brothers in the community because we share everything—our joys and our suffering.

*A feminist and free thinker, Salomé Costa longs to study theology and, if the Catholic church allowed, would seek to become a priest. Like many other people of faith with few material resources, her education comes mostly from Bible meetings, grassroots workshops and seminars. Salomé is very active in the church community of Christo Mestre in the eastern part of São Paulo's periphery.*

*Salomé struggled with tuberculosis for many years and today has only one lung. She lives with her sister and has never married. I met with Salomé Costa on a sunny Sunday afternoon at an ecumenical celebration of the Bible.*

*Although Salomé hasn't studied formal theology, she claims to speak the theology of "daily life itself." In the summer of 1990 she was invited to participate in a national meeting of sixty-seven women theologians. She recounts, "They spoke above my head, but as incredible as it seems, I didn't feel diminished by their*

While attending an ecumenical celebration held in a local park, Salomé wears a bright pink T-shirt that reads, "Woman, the freedom of your people also depends on your struggle."

*knowledge. They have intellectual understanding, but I have the practice, the experience!"*

*Salomé's experience of the Catholic church in São Paulo has been strongly affected by the 1990 "shake-up" when the archdiocese of São Paulo was divided-up according to Vatican orders. This decision not only weakened the influence of Cardinal Paulo Evaristo Arns, a staunch defender of human rights, but also divided the city more along rich-poor lines and was a severe blow to the local CEBs. In Salomé's sub-diocese, the dynamic Franciscan bishop, Dom Angélico Sandalo Bernadino, was replaced by a more traditional-style bishop, Dom Fernando Legal, who has severely restricted the expression of lay leadership in the region.*

༄ ༄ ༄

I grew up in a remote part of the state Mato Grosso [Amazon basin area] and worked the fields until I was eighteen. We were five sisters and two brothers.

Then I became sick with tuberculosis and was hospitalized for four years—far away from my family. I could never move back to the countryside because I needed to see the doctor often.

When I became ill, I began to reflect more on the Bible. I started to discover the commitment that my parents made when they baptized me as a child.

Our baptism is a commitment!

Each time we discover the commitment we have as Christians, we can no longer say, "I go to church to find peace." I don't think I'll find much peace there! Because, when you know that someone doesn't have food, another doesn't have a house, it creates a conflict inside of you.

We do encounter the strength of God in church, but it's not this peaceful peace that keeps you quiet and sends you home. And the God we encounter inspires us to struggle against these things that create conflict! We're struggling so that others can have peace—housing and work and food. We're searching for life itself.

You see, the Reign of God has to start right here.

When no one has food, when no one has a house, when no one can go to school—then the Reign of God isn't happening! God

Cardinal Paulo Evaristo Arns (R) presides at the installation of Bishop Fernando Legal (L), May 28, 1989.

is present when we search for these things here and now. That's how the Reign of God begins!

❧ ❧ ❧

When I was in the hospital with tuberculosis, I lost both of my parents. My mother suffered from mental problems since I was ten years old. And my father died of cancer four months after she did. Then my two brothers also died.

But when people ask, "Do you live alone in São Paulo?" I answer, "No, I have a very *big* family! It grows all the time!" I really feel that we are sisters and brothers in the community because we share everything—our joys and our suffering.

I don't feel loneliness. No. These people are my family.

I think when you feel suffering in your own skin, you can either become discouraged and think everything's over, or you can become more animated in the common struggle for life.

I've been involved with the church for twenty-five years—that's half of my life!

Not just attending mass, which I've done since I was a child, but participating, especially in the small communities. I lead Bible meetings and liturgies, and participate in the formation of lay ministers. I also work with the grassroots movements—especially the struggle for health care, day care and women's groups.

In the CEBs we don't just listen to the priest preach, but we participate in the Word. That is, we can't stay just praying inside of the church.

Some churches, especially the Pentecostals, tell the people not to participate in the grassroots struggle! They think that the church alone is everything, that the Reign of God is only within, that life is only praying, only spiritual.

No, we have to have *action*. We have to go outside of the church to search for life! This is in the Gospel.

"The struggle" is the survival of the people. Through the struggle we discover the strength we have. We are searching for life. For survival. And no one is going to "donate" this life to us. If we sit around waiting for it, it will come too late.

We have to search for it and claim it!

You see, a small group of people dominate our system—the business people with all the wealth in their hands. And the great masses of poor people aren't aware! Once we discover that we're important as persons, we'll begin to struggle.

That's how we'll get out of poverty!

And we don't see such differences with other religions because we're *all* searching for life! Schools, transportation, a hospital—we *share* these things together! It's so good to work together with other churches!

ᢞᢞ ᢞᢞ ᢞᢞ

We call our Bible meetings "street groups."

We go out of the church and into the streets to gather families and reflect on the Bible in the light of our lives. And the situation of our lives is horrible!

In the *favela*, one tiny hut has twelve or fifteen people living in it. It's awful! To have food, the mother has to work, and many women are single mothers because the men leave them, so she has to leave her children unattended, and then the children get into trouble with drugs and street life.

These are really big problems.

In the Word of God you discover that these things aren't right. For example, you discover your street isn't paved. So, the street group animates the neighborhood people to struggle for this improvement. We don't only pray with the families, but we *do* things —together.

You see, when you discover faith, you're involved in politics. That is, when you are searching for *life*, you're engaged in a political act.

The poor are so marginalized and exploited by the politics of the government! So, the church should be involved in politics in this sense: walking with the people who are searching to improve their lives, searching for the life of God.

Reading the Gospels has always encouraged me.

In the Gospels we discover that God is always on the side of the poorest, the most marginalized, those who don't have any value in society's eyes. Jesus testified to this with his whole life.

This is what happens in the church!

In the small community of poor people we feel the presence of God because we know each others' lives and struggles. We can continue without getting discouraged.

My hope is that we always dwell in this faith. In this struggle. Faith and struggle. The church provides the communion we need to go out and struggle for what we need to live.

ᢞᢞ ᢞᢞ ᢞᢞ

The struggle is right here in our own neighborhood—there is so much violence against women!

There was a man near here throwing acid on women's legs just because they wore mini-skirts! That is, women don't even have the freedom to dress as they wish! Some friends of mine were victims of this. Lately there's another character with a pocket knife jabbing women!

Women also suffer terrible injustice inside of the church.

For example, it's the women who lead celebrations and animate the CEBs, but when it is a celebration of Mass, the Bishop says women can't even read the Gospel! But it's women who evangelize! They're the ones walking with the communities!

A recent example is a celebration where we commissioned the lay ministers, and the Bishop said that women couldn't preach the Gospel. We had to have a deacon read it!

There are all these barriers—even barriers to the sacred.

For example, we know that in our church, women can't consecrate the bread and wine—yet it's women who bring life into this world! Women are almost always responsible for raising children! Women care for life—right?

I believe this will change, starting with each woman who begins to know how to struggle, who knows that she has rights, that she's *not* impure, that she is responsible for life. I don't think I'm impure. I don't think I can't celebrate or share in this sacred moment.

I believe that things can change, but we may have to struggle for a long time!

This is why I belong to a woman's group. We give value to women because they are engaged in everything from the grassroots movements to the churches. If one day you took women out of the CEBs, they'd fold up!

It's sad to see in our group that married women sometimes lose their freedom. Sometimes they can't even talk to other men! I think I have more freedom without a husband. I come and go with freedom—I love freedom!

But we aren't totally free because of how we were educated. We grew up being taught, "Women can't do this, women can't do that." As much as we want to free ourselves, this oppression seems to be rooted deep inside of us.

I have a friend, an incredible person, who participates in the grassroots movement. Her husband finally said, "You have to choose between the church and me!" She said, "But I want both!" And she kept right on! With time, he got better—he just had to understand.

Sometimes you see wonderfully aware women whose husbands never let them participate, so they stay tied to their husband, house and children. This can create huge conflicts in the home. Thank God I don't have this!

Women still don't have many opportunities in society.

Here I am, fifty years old, with no means to live on! It's worse if you don't have a profession. But the more you know, the more you discover the rights you have. You learn to participate and change things.

I belong to a group of women who sew. Through our conversations, we learn about each other's problems. When women say they can't leave their houses because their husbands won't let them, I always say to the women, "Don't let your husband treat you like an object. You are important!"

I really love this work!

ʝɞ ʝɞ ʝɞ

*What do you think about the Vatican-ordered changes in São Paulo, including the replacement of your bishop, Angélico, with Bishop Fernando Legal?*

It isn't very good! We don't know this new bishop very well, but he doesn't seem to be very open or committed to the social struggle like Dom Angélico was. Dom Angélico denounced injustices from his position, he struggled alongside the people. This animated the people! We see this new bishop as more on the side of just the "spiritual"—you see?

It really seems things have receded a bit. The lay ministry is suffering. Our space within the church is being eliminated.

Maybe if the people join together we can change this.

*What changes would you like to see in the structure of power in Rome?*

I'd like to see them consult the CEBs much more. As it is, they don't have anything to do with the people! The people live in poverty. Sometimes people are so poor that they don't have the energy to even know that they have a spirit.

Only when we speak from the *base* itself will we have participation.

In the crowded Tiradentes housing complex in the periphery of São Paulo, CEB member Eurides Cruz Nunes leads a Sunday liturgy, using hosts already consecrated by a priest.

*Do you think people who are born on the wealthier and more privileged side of society also need God's liberation?*

Well, I think rich people have a great emptiness. In spite of having and buying everything, if they don't share their wealth, they'll feel very empty.

We hear about people that are able to study and possess everything, then they're not satisfied, they turn to drugs and other things. Their wealth doesn't fill their emptiness. I think that there wouldn't be this emptiness, there wouldn't be this division between classes if people shared.

Rich people who have everything also feel empty of God because God doesn't want people to accumulate without sharing, God doesn't want people exploiting other people. Those who are very rich have exploited people. If a businessman owns a factory and pays the workers a dignified wage, he won't accumulate as much wealth. He will have shared the profits.

But, the Gospel says how difficult it is for a rich person to save him or herself. Rich people don't want to share, they only want to donate out of their surplus.

It isn't a sin to have wealth if you share your goods.

*If you could say anything to these privileged people, what would you say to them?*

I think you have to be committed to the poorest class, those who don't even have the opportunity to study. You should be open to help the people who are most poor—who are searching for the right to life. Find those people who don't even have a voice! Be the voice for the voiceless!

If you look at the Gospel, you'll discover that God is always on the side of the smallest. So we never feel alone. We're always in the presence of God. I am a home of God! God is present in each one of us! God comes to us, and uses us to *serve* others. Yes, we must allow God to work through us to serve others.

I pray that we always feel this presence of God in our lives.

# 3

# EDILSON HERCULANO DA SILVA

The rulers in our country want power and riches even if it means that we live in misery.

I go back to how Christ looked at the world. He was a person on the side of the people—rich as well as poor. He spoke of faith and love, but denounced injustice.

I believe the church should be this way too, denouncing every injustice against the people.

*I met Edilson Herculano on my first trip as an adult to Brazil in 1987, and visited with him on my two subsequent trips, in1989 and 1990. At first, he lived in a small, simple home in the neighborhood of Nossa Senhora Aparecida on the periphery of São Paulo where he managed a small broom-making cooperative that employed neighborhood youths. At the time of our next visit, three years later, he had built a new home, was working in a religious bookstore, and was more outspoken than ever about the rights and dignity of people living in the favela.*

*Perhaps the greatest change during those three years occurred inside of the church, for Edilson lives in the same subdiocese as Salomé. For Edilson and other lay leaders, the work at the base continues in spite of the great vacuum existing where there once was a guiding vision and support from Bishop Angélico. Edilson has hope because he believes that even for the new Bishop, Fernando Legal, conversion is always possible. Recalling*

Edilson stands outside of his home while two of his three children look out of the front gate. On the wall is a campaign poster for the Workers' Party candidate for Governor.

31

*the story of the people of El Salvador who "woke up" Archbishop Oscar Romero, Edilson insists, "The faith of our people can also convert a bishop!"*

ᴪᴈ ᴪᴈ ᴪᴈ

I've been living in Nossa Senhora Aparecida in the eastern zone of São Paulo for fifteen years.

I'm glad to have a secure salary from the Paulist bookstore to support my family, but you can become a prisoner to that kind of work. I wish I had the freedom to work in the community—organizing people, teaching literacy, working in the CEB and doing consciousness-raising. This is a real dilemma for me—having to support a family I love, yet wanting the freedom to work with the people.

I've been very involved with the local church—teaching catechesis, planning liturgies, leading celebrations and helping with the youth group.

ᴪᴈ ᴪᴈ ᴪᴈ

The situation of the poor in this *favela* is full of suffering.

We came from far away regions because we didn't have the means to survive there. Our lands were seized and we were driven out, forced to come to the big cities. We have nowhere to live in São Paulo except the *favelas* or under the viaducts.

Because of this, we suffer a lot of discrimination.

People say, "They're thieves! They're scoundrels! They're illiterate!"

This really messes up our lives.

It creates a barrier between us and the rest of society that's a little better off.

The *favela* of Nossa Senhora Aparecida, looking out on the main street, near Edilson's home.

They consider us the slum but we call our neighborhood a *vila* (small town or borough) because we want to change things!

A slum isn't accepted by the neighbors. Even people who are so poor that they don't have enough to eat, but who pay rent, discriminate against the people of the *favela*!

Imagine, they think that because you live in the *favela* you have no intelligence or ability. I sometimes begin to feel this myself! No wonder people aren't waking up to join the struggle!

Young girls and boys feel this discrimination also.

They are treated like hoodlums. They have to date within the town or people say, "You're dating a girl from the *favela*! She's no good! No one there is any good!"

Imagine—the young people carry this inside their heads!

*ᢥ ᢥ ᢥ*

One of our hopes in our little town is to build a community.

We believe that since God is really in the midst of the poor, we can work to obtain a better life. In the CEB, we meet together and look to God to liberate us from all of our problems.

The Bible is the most important part of our journey. We link it with our current reality and identify with past peoples—especially the enslaved. For example, in our neighborhood we see that our reality is very harsh. The book of Exodus is similar to our journey today. The people of God were in slavery under Pharaoh who crushed them and even killed children so they would not revolt against him.

This is still happening! We are a people enslaved by the powerful ones here in Brazil and we need God to liberate us.

*ᢥ ᢥ ᢥ*

On the feast of Corpus Christi, bishops, priests, nuns and lay people march in the streets of São Paulo under a banner supporting labor unions, "A worker outside of a union is like a needle in a haystack". Bishop Angélico, who in 1990 was replaced by the more traditional Bishop Legal, marches in the front row of the clergy (the robed man to the left). June 21, 1987.

It's such a hard life here!

We have so many problems—poor roads, no sewage, rodents, and so much violence. The violence is induced by the very structure of our country! There are vigilantes in the town who are prepared to kill people—those they think steal or use drugs.

So many people killing one another! But you see, the very problem of sanitation—the lack of plumbing and trash collection—is also a violence against our people.

It's so easy to become exhausted. But it used to be worse!

Through the strength that the church provides, we've managed to get running water, lights, trash collection and some plumbing. The church doesn't form a group to do this for us—it teaches us to organize ourselves to struggle and win these improvements.

The church is really like a light for us. It's a church that stands on our side.

It understands our reality and our suffering, and seeks to help as much as it can. Because the church walks together with us, we can hope our neighborhood really will improve.

ॐ ॐ ॐ

In the beginning, the lack of a priest was a problem for us.

So we began to organize ourselves.

Now, our liturgy team celebrates the Word of God, looking more and more on our own reality. Today we actually celebrate our reality more than a Mass in the traditional sense. We make a liturgy of the life of the people, connecting it with God.

Today, we've broken from our total dependence on a priest. If a priest comes now, it's for baptisms, marriages or a big feast day. But the community itself works just fine with a sister or a lay missioner.

The majority of people involved with the church are women, which is difficult and painful for me. Where are my brothers? At celebrations, there are twenty or thirty women and only five men! This is our "participation!"

I don't know why this is so. Maybe because of our *machista* ideology. Maybe men feel embarrassed or diminished by participating in the church. And maybe women are trying to liberate themselves from the men's machismo, so they participate all the more, which is good.

It's complicated. I just wish it weren't so.

彩 彩 彩

Community is so important because individualism is such a great problem in our world.

In opting for the poor, the Brazilian church is becoming less individualistic. Our life in the CEBs teaches us that if we live just as individuals, we'll fall even deeper into misery. As the people at the base who are suffering the most, we seek the God that *unites* people to help us resolve our problems together.

And if the church continues to opt for a Brazil of sisters and brothers, if it continues to preach the option for the poor, then Brazil may be transformed!

We may one day bring an end to the misery.

But it's only through the church and faith in God that Brazil will change. Through the politicians—no way!

The root of the problems afflicting us is avarice. The powerful people—those seeking only their profit and greatness—are blocking this change. They want equality with other powerful countries, but don't want equality *inside* of Brazil.

Brazil is a super rich country with conditions to give everyone a quality life. But our rulers make billions of dollars exporting arms, while killing their own people with hunger and exploitation. This is absurd!

I go back to how Christ looked at the world. He was a person on the side of the people—rich as well as poor. He spoke of faith and love, but denounced injustice.

I've come to believe that the Church should be this way too, denouncing every injustice against the people.

彩 彩 彩

*What are the effects of the change in bishops in your area, the replacing of Dom Angélico with Dom Fernando Legal?*

This whole situation is a really big blow to us. These new appointments and the splitting of the archdiocese have shaken São Paulo and even all of Brazil! Perhaps the Pope is being pressured by those who fear how strong the church of liberation is becoming here.

Edilson working at the broom factory cooperative
in his neighborhood of Nossa Senhora Aparecida.

It's only been one year since we've had the new bishop. The advances we've made in lay ministry are cooling down a bit. But we're still hoping that things will change.

*Does a new bishop make that much difference to the journey of the CEBs?*

We have three important groups that are interconnected in their work with the CEBs—the people, the priests and the bishop.

First, the people themselves—those in the church of liberation and engaged in transformation—won't forget the advances we've made. Next are the priests who are very invested in the church of the CEBs. Their commitment is harder to sustain because they know they lack support from the bishop. Then come the bishops—but a bishop alone won't do anything! That is, it's up to the people and the priests to continue these progressive and liberating advances. And our priests are fairly radical.

So, as the people and the priests work together, there will be continuity in the work, sometimes in spite of the bishops.

*Do you have hope for the future of the CEBs then?*

Yes. I have very much hope, yes. I have hope because we see that conversion happens. The arrival of this new bishop, Dom Fernando Legal, to our region can be the occasion for his conversion!

Like what happened with Archbishop Oscar Romero—right? After the people woke him up, he gave up his life, and Romero is living today in our midst. This can also happen in our region! I have much hope in the people, our communities—they can convert our bishop!

*What can people outside of Brazil do to be in solidarity with your struggles?*

First, the U.S. should pull out of other countries and stop their political scheming to get so much of our goods. With the intelligence and education that people there have, the U.S. could really help carry a rich message to other countries. Please, be in solidarity with our Brazilian reality. Help us. See us as a country that needs to survive. A country that needs to be transformed. We need you and believe that you really need us also.

*If you could speak directly to people in the First World, what would you say to them?*

I want to congratulate people who are resisters! Resisting the oppression that is very strong inside the U.S.

I also ask you all to believe very much that God came to liberate us and will unite us one day in a much broader struggle, all together, before all oppressive structures that live for money and power.

I want to tell our wealthy brothers and sisters that salvation doesn't come only for the poor, but, yes, for the rich as well. Because of this, I plead that you all share a little! Share a little bit of your wealth, your happiness, your knowledge with our suffering, exploited people so that tomorrow we, too, may smile a little bit, so that tomorrow we, too, could have a society that's a little more equal.

I also believe that the poor have a lot to share with the rich. I believe that the poor have more to share with the rich than the rich have to share with the poor! Our God is so marvelous that whoever walks with God has everything to share with everyone!

Whoever walks only for himself dies without leaving regret in anyone's heart.

# 4

## GORETH BARRADAS

My house is always full, because people in the countryside say, "So and so is sick, send them to Marabá and tell them to find Goreth. She'll find a way to help!"

I don't have fixed employment, but people always find a way to provide. I work for the love of people who suffer, especially children.

When you work for money alone, love doesn't exist.

*I met and interviewed Goreth Barradas in 1987, when I spent a month in her neighborhood, Liberdade ("Liberty"), in Marabá, Pará. Later, while traveling through the Amazon basin on pastoral visits to the CEBs, Goreth and I became fast friends and soulmates.*

*Goreth's city of Marabá, not far from gold and iron ore mines, is a boom town bursting at the seams with violence and slave-like labor. Goreth was born in 1959 to an Indigenous family. During this period when white settlers were invading Pará, settlers kidnapped the infant Goreth, murdered her family and raised her as their own. Only as an adult did Goreth discover the whole truth of this terrible history.*

*Today Goreth's own home is abuzz with three children left to her care, three younger half-brothers, an ailing grandmother and welcomed strangers. Active in the local base community, Goreth founded Liberdade's youth group, started a women's group, is active in the land movement and works as an advocate for children and the elderly. She also works with SERPAJ (Serviço Paz e*

Goreth does the daily laundry in her back yard
with water from her well.

*Justiça or Peace and Justice Service)—the Latin American move-
ment for nonviolent social change founded by Nobel Prize-winner
Perez Esquivel—attending and giving workshops to SERPAJ
groups throughout her region.*

*Sitting in small, battered school desks, we talk in the neigh-
borhood's one-room community building. Even with children play-
ing outside and peeking in the door, it is the most privacy we can
find. A true good Samaritan, she explains the motivation of her life
ministry simply, "I feel the pain of others." For Goreth, this is the
message of the Gospel.*

҂ ҂ ҂

I can't remember very much of my history, but this is the little I remember.

Before 1958, only Indigenous lived in Marabá.

Then the white people began to invade to extract rubber and
kill jaguars for their skins. They also robbed and killed many Indians. "Marabá" is an Indian word that means "worthless"—referring to the children of white people who raped Indians.

Sometimes the settlers would kill the parents and take the
little children to the city to raise them. That's what happened to
me. But I was so little, I couldn't remember!

Growing-up, I would look at myself among other people and
I always felt different, always asked, "Who am I?" I knew there
was something wrong—even in how my parents mistreated and
shamed me among my siblings.

Three years ago I discovered who I am, thanks to a priest,
Father José, who works with the Indians. I confessed to him some
memories, and he pieced together the truth. It isn't a coincidence
that my story happened in so many villages! I discovered the
Indians didn't give up hope of finding me one day. The white
people killed my mother, my father, and my tiny brother because
he bit them.

I remember this because, when I was eight, I overheard a
conversation between my "parents" about what happened. I carried all this deep inside me until I was twenty-nine years old.

One day my friend Father José brought me before the Indians to find the sign on my body, the mark that only they would
recognize. A very old, old woman found it by putting her finger
on my head.

Still, I've learned to love my family. In spite of everything, I owe them my life.

My "brothers" were born later. They will never know the truth about all this—I've made myself hide it so as not to hurt or trouble them. I've kept this so many years!

It's only the boys' father I don't like. I'm enraged at him for what he did. I can only hope to understand this atrocity and make other people aware so that it doesn't happen again.

ЯЯ ЯЯ ЯЯ

I was only able to go to school until I was seventeen.

Since then, I've been formed by grassroots courses. I've studied theology and anthropology, and I've participated in union meetings, the landless movement and law courses. Really, my formation comes mostly from the Gospels!

Six years ago, I began working with the church. My friend Toinha and I started a youth group, raising consciousness among the young people so they wouldn't get involved in drugs or prostitution. Being a church youth group doesn't just mean having church meetings, but struggling for a better world.

For two years, I earned half of a minimum wage working for the Archdiocese of Marabá in remote rural villages. Father Renato, a great supporter of our community, and I would walk for miles and miles on foot, with packs on our backs, to arrive in villages and animate the CEBs.

I learned to love this people! Today they're like family to me!

Now, when someone in the backlands gets sick, where there's no clinic and they don't have relatives in the city, they come to me, stay in my house, sometimes for weeks until we finally get medical help.

My house is always full, because the villagers say, "So and so is sick, send them to Marabá and tell them to find Goreth. She'll find a way to help!"

Goreth cares for her sick grandmother, whose room is decorated with political posters for Workers' Party candidates. Now conscious of her indigenous roots, Goreth wears a T-shirt announcing a campaign to defend the survival of the Javari Indians.

I don't merely take people to the doctor, I conscientize[†] them as we go, telling them that one day we have to change this situation, because it is a priority that all human beings have a doctor, health care, and food.

When people come to me suffering, I suffer with them. I wait with them in long lines and say "This isn't right."

Every moment I am in these painful situations, I know: *I will never be silent.* I may not see the world free before I die, but at least I can touch others who will help this come about.

🙞 🙞 🙞

I work mostly with old people and children.

They're so alike because they are the people who most need affection and care, yet they're the most looked down on.

Old people work their whole lives and have to beg to survive. In Marabá there are five or six elderly people begging on every corner. This is why I feel so much for my eighty-two year old grandmother. I've been taking care of her for three years, though I can barely afford to buy her milk. Social Security isn't enough to survive on and it's so hard to obtain!

One day I was at the Social Security office to get some information, and I saw an old woman there signing up for benefits. The manager was so cruel to her, grabbing her arm brutally, shoving her to sit down.

This shook me to the depths!

I got up and said, "Why are you doing that to her?" He said, "Who are you to talk to me that way?" I said, "I'm no one, just a human being with a heart. But since you get a salary here, you're obliged to treat people well! It doesn't cost anything to treat people with respect!"

---

[†]In Brazil, the verb *conscientizar,* translated as "to conscientize," refers to the process of human beings achieving critical consciousness—awareness of both their socio-cultural reality and their capacity to transform that reality. The process of *conscientização,* or conscientization, was articulated in the pedagogical method of Brazilian educator Paulo Freire and later popularized by Brazilian archbishop Dom Hélder Câmara.

He grabbed me and threatened to call the police.

I left there so hurt and angry. Yet it was his rudeness that brought me to the cause of the elderly! From then on, Toinha and I have been working to help old people get their Social Security.

These people are so poor! I want the people to organize themselves. I want to educate them to vote for a better manager, better services for retired people, clean drinking water at the office. Now, it's a scandal, a total injustice!

But when the poor elderly people try to give me a few cents, I say "I don't want this." You see, I don't do this work for pay.

In my work, I never think of the future—what I'll eat or wear tomorrow. Even today, I don't have fixed employment, but people always find a way to provide. I work for the love of people who suffer, especially children.

When you work for money alone, love doesn't exist.

ॐ ॐ ॐ

The suffering of my people has drawn me into working with them for change. So much suffering and violence over the land!

Death itself!

In the countryside the large landowners send gunmen to kill peasants and remove them from the land. Thousands have died! We have so much unused land, while whole families walk the sidewalks dying of hunger.

Yet I think the biggest root of all oppressions afflicting Brazil is found in the media, because they put such beautiful images before the people.

They become addicted to TV, truly addicted. This enslaves people!

Every night the soap operas end in such suspense that people say, "I have to watch tomorrow. Something important will happen!" But nothing new happens. They even say, "I'm not going to church. I can't go to that meeting because of the show on tonight."

The media becomes a weapon that represses the people.

But the people don't feel repressed. They feel happy because they're watching a soap opera—where men are always having affairs with two or three women, and people always win without struggling. People begin to think everything will come to them without work!

If you're poor, you see all that luxury on TV and you want to imitate it. This is a horrible education for our children!

This isn't by chance, but by plan.

The government is afraid of the Catholic church. Not the church itself, but the grassroots movements—the people who *are* the church. The movements threaten the government because the people in them don't agree to slave wages and oppression.

When the people are hooked on TV, they're so absorbed that they forget what's happening around them. They end up blind. They look but don't see.

This truly oppresses people. They become parasites.

Yet it's a "peaceful" oppression because people don't feel oppressed.

❦ ❦ ❦

The injustice, violence and oppression in Brazil will only end with a nonviolent struggle at the base, tearing down the structures above us.

Our faith gives us hope that one day things will improve.

Not by standing back, but by entering the struggle.

The greatest sorrows in my life are when a child dies without medical care, or when an old person dies without even getting into a hospital. I've seen elderly people fall on the floor, begging for help, and the doctor doesn't even look.

Sometimes, when I see things like this, I feel like I don't want to live anymore.

But the people give me strength for the struggle.

I learned to love the people and they help me. They teach me through their suffering, through their joyful smiles. They're very, very humble people. They give me strength to walk.

❦ ❦ ❦

Truly, my work is raising awareness of the Gospel—the Gospel in the life of the suffering, massacred people. We work so that through the Gospel we can all struggle for liberation from hunger, from a salary of misery, from all that oppresses the Brazilian people.

I try to show people what Christ asked of us—that we denounce the oppressors, struggle for freedom and break the chains of those who live in bondage. And the chains we see today are hunger, misery and oppression.

Before, the Church said of our suffering, "It's the will of God." Today they see that God doesn't want people to suffer, suffer, suffer.

Today we believe we should struggle for change.

The problem in the church today is that they don't spend money for lay people to work at the grassroots.

For example, the Archdiocese of Marabá gave me a scholarship for a theology course in Belém for lay leaders, but I didn't even have enough money to buy food and water along the way!

Even among the priests who preach liberation and who denounce violence against women, this one priest still made us sign a release that if there was an accident on our way to work with the rural CEBs, the diocese wouldn't be responsible for us. Imagine!

After that, I said I'd never work directly with a priest again. Yes, with the people. Yes, with the church. But with priests, no. Not without their true support. Not unless they truly respect lay people and women.

Basically, they don't pay what they preach: a just salary.

This will only change when we demand respect and dignity.

ॐ ॐ ॐ

Father Renato, the priest who always accompanied us in our struggle and who built up the CEBs in the Amazon, recently moved to Nicaragua. The new priest isn't a priest of the people! He's only a priest to say Mass. He doesn't organize the people.

For me, a church that doesn't speak about politics isn't a church, because our lives are politics! There are rich people exploiting and poor people suffering. This is politics!

You see, when you're well off, you don't concern yourself with those who are in trouble. This is a matter of not having faith—of not knowing or living the Gospel.

In the past, the church itself was like this. We know that any religion or church exists for only one of two reasons—to oppress or to liberate.

In the past, the people only said "amen" with no right to comment on the Gospel. Today the church lives the Gospel, the people participate, the people do the Eucharist, they celebrate life, suffering, happiness in their liturgies.

Ultimately, the most important thing isn't religion, but a commitment with God and with the people, even if you don't know who God is.

Today the church is turning towards liberation. For us, liberation theology is the point where a friend dies for a just cause, for an oppressed person. Their blood is like a seed among the people. It's the leaven for a new life that will grow, a seed that will be born again.

This gives us hope!

My hope is to someday see a country that's well-governed, to see all children with the right to school, health and play. I want to see every street child with a home to live in, where they can be joyful and live happily.

Personally, my future is in the three children that I'm raising. All that I do is so that they will study and have a critical consciousness about right and wrong.

I want my children to be someone in life.

Free people with their hearts turned toward humanity.

One day we will see true justice, when everyone eats from the same plate—rich, poor, Indians, whites. A new earth.

ॐ ॐ ॐ

*Describe your work with the women in your neighborhood.*

In our women's group, we share our experiences—some women were prostitutes with horrible lives, and some now have companions. The most important thing in our meetings is confidentiality. We also share recipes and joke around a lot!

For several years Goreth assisted Father Renato Barth, S.J., in the work of forming CEBs in remote Amazon villages. Here Fr. Renato celebrates multiple baptisms in a village where priestly visits are rare. Not only are there few priests to serve the many people, but the rough mud roads to the village become flooded during the rainy season.

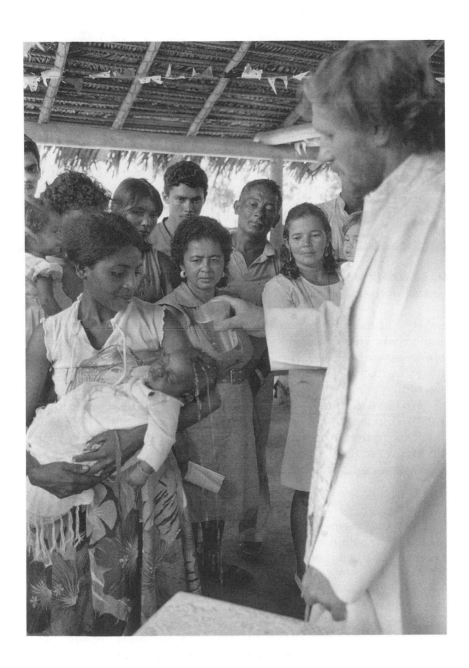

I'm so moved by the courage and strength of these women. I'm not ashamed to share my own experiences. I was also used and abused. We've been used for the pleasure of men, like cheap objects that aren't worth anything! Women don't have the right to speak, to decide, to anything—except listening.

We also try to become more aware of how we educate our own children, so that what happened to us won't happen to them. We were raised so that the brother rules over the sister. We help our friends to raise their children as equals, since we're all children of God. This is even in the Bible—God created Eve not from Adam's foot, but from the rib, for women to walk side by side with men. This means as equals.

*Do you think your life is more free without a spouse or father telling you what to do?*

It would be better to have a companion—I mean, a companion who would never mistreat me. I am a free woman; no one will ever bind me. If I find a companion, he'll have to accept me as I am, just as I'll have to get to know him and conscientize him.

We have various married women friends who are suffering so much. This is why the women's movement exists—to rescue our image of women. And women need to learn and pass it on to men. We aren't struggling against men, for separation. We want men to see women as women, as human beings.

*You said that people are participating more in the life of the church. Does this also cause conflict in a church where some leaders don't want lay participation?*

It seems so. According to some, the Pope thinks priests are like saints who function to say Mass. In the end, priests are human beings, just like me! The priest is a sinner. I don't see why we treat them so differently. We should all be equal because God is equal. God is man, God is woman, God is black, is white, is Indian, is Brazilian, is a foreigner!

So, really, everyone should be a priest. We already have married people giving out the Eucharist consecrated by the priest. If the Gospel says God is in the least of these, God is in every person—man, woman, old, black, white, married.

*What's the biggest challenge confronting the Catholic church today?*

Protestantism, that is, the growth of *creentes* ["believers"] or Pentecostals, these fanatics that see the Bible as a rigid model, teaching people to just put up with the rest of reality outside the Bible. The *creentes* propose an easy road for people—*only* singing, *only* praying, *only* shouting without being concerned about your neighbor. People will choose what's easy, right?

But, if you choose the road of crying with the one who cries, shouting with the one who shouts, risking prison with someone being imprisoned, this is more difficult. I have chosen this road, but it is very, very difficult.

There are days when I don't sleep. I leave before sunrise and return at night. When someone gets sick, I go with them to the hospital in the middle of the night. I'm available all the time. If I were a *creente*, I'd sleep all night without concern for anyone because Jesus will take care of everything!

I think the best way to respond is to work at the base, call meetings, show solidarity and show people that they aren't alone, that they have someone who will suffer *with* them, they have someone who will try to *stop* their suffering.

*What can people outside of Brazil do to be in solidarity with the people of Brazil?*

We really, really need your help to protect the environment. As long as your money goes to our government, it won't help anything. Your money should create employment. For example, the gold miners pollute the water with mercury and destroy nature because they can't earn enough to support their families.

Invest in the grassroots movements. The people who protect the environment are the people that live from the land—Indigenous, farmers, the rubber-tappers!

Another message is to search for true information, because the news we get from the TV, newspapers and radio never present the real problems. They never tell the real history of the people. We need teams to research Brazil, listen to the grassroots movements, see the lands being burned and see who's really provoking the massacre of the Brazilian rainforest.

*What message would you give to people who are already engaged in the struggle for peace and justice?*

Sometimes people aren't aware of what's going on, but they have the desire and feel with others in their hearts. They know that the poor feel just like they do. This is the greatest message: *to feel human.* If you like to be happy, to smile, and see someone who is sad, you only have to look to see that the other person also wants to smile and be joyful! Whether they are black or white, foreigners or Americans—they cry and laugh like you do!

From the moment you really feel it in your own skin—when you pinch yourself, it hurts—then you'll remember that if you pinch someone else, they also hurt. This resolves the problem. It comes down to feeling what others feel.

Also, people who have power should know that power comes from the people, the suffering people. If everyone was equal, no one would live in misery.

*Is there anything else you want to say to people in the North?*

Sincerely, though we hear of the U.S. as one of the nations that oppresses Brazil, it isn't only the U.S.—it's oppressive people within our own nation.

It's painful for us to know that the people of the U.S. have power in their hands while thousands of children die of hunger, old people are abandoned, and the poor suffer. I'm certain that people there could help out in many ways—except through exploitation.

Above all, people should believe in God. We can't make a universe or give the very gift of life. Surely there's a superior being!

I wonder about those who say they don't believe in God. What do they believe in? They have to believe in something! What is it? Some people believe in money and live as if money is God. But that's not true.

God isn't money or power. God carries our image, our likeness.

# 5

# TOINHA LIMA BARROS

I believe it's impossible for someone to have a conversion to God without having a conversion to the poor. God preached liberation for the poor, so ours is a God of the poor and oppressed.

We know that the rich aren't liberated. They are often slaves to money, ambition, power. And their money makes them slaves to fear. Equality for all people is liberation from fear!

*I first met and interviewed Toinha in 1987, when she was twenty-four. A friend and neighbor of Goreth, Toinha's astute political savvy punctuates nearly every one of our conversations. Having achieved the equivalent of a high school education, Toinha was then trained through church seminars and grassroots courses.*

*Toinha's primary occupation is teaching high school in her neighborhood of Liberdade, but her commitments extend far beyond one job. She is a leader in the grassroots church and has long worked with SERPAJ. She is also active in the Marabá teachers' union and helped found the local Worker's Party. With Goreth Barradas, she has helped to establish neighborhood youth groups and women's groups, and also teaches catechesis in two neighborhoods. More recently, she is becoming a strong advocate for the elderly and marginalized children of Marabá.*

*Toinha dreams of opening a literacy school in her neighborhood, Liberdade, using Paulo Freire's consciousness-raising method.[†] Unfortunately, she barely earns enough money to put food on the table for herself and her adopted daughter.*

Toinha and her adopted daughter, Mayra. The poster reads: "Woman—No to Discrimination!"

*Living in the Amazon basin, Toinha is profoundly aware of the environmental devastation surrounding her. The day before our interview, Toinha and her students marched in Maraba's Independence Day parade, carrying banners in defense of the environment. The police chased and started to beat up one of her students who carried a sign denouncing violence against rural workers.*

ৡ ৡ ৡ

I was born in Marabá. We lived in the interior and I came to the city to study. How I wish had a college degree! I would love to contribute more to this society through study!

Our life is really difficult. Like many others in this neighborhood, we're poor.

In my family, I'm the only one who got to go to school. My mother works as a maid, and my father, who was murdered two years ago, worked the fields.

Since his death, our family is starting a new life and it's not easy.

I earn only a minimum wage as a teacher—forty-two dollars a month! This makes it hard to support five people!

In our neighborhood we've just started to organize a movement of the elderly and a women's group. I've also tried to organize a group for black people here.

I'm not very black, but I must be black! If I stood beside a white person, I couldn't call myself white. I'm not an Indian, and there isn't another race here—so I must be black!

This is Brazil! So many colors, and no one wanting to admit they're black! There's still so much prejudice.

Sometimes black people themselves are ashamed to join a black group—they have the mind of the dominant ideology and

---

†Paulo Freire is a Brazilian educational philosopher who invented the technique of "conscientization" or consciousness-raising literacy and education. This method empowers the student to both understand his or her reality and creatively act to change it. The CEBs borrow heavily from this method.

Toinha (l.) leads a women's meeting where neighbors gather to share their struggles and encourage one another.

say, "This black thing is nonsense!" You see, in the soap operas the princess is always white, the rich person is white, and the maid is black.

We have a long way to go.

ॐ ॐ ॐ

When I was fourteen I entered the Assembly of God Church. I stayed for two years—then I couldn't take it any more.

People were saying that it was a sin to wear make-up and short skirts, yet so many people around us were illiterate, dying without medical care, dying of hunger! No one said this was a sin!

Then, when I was eighteen, I met Father Renato, a companion who opened my eyes to the way of justice.

At the time, people from Marabá were occupying the neighborhood of Liberdade. It was a tough battle. We fought with the police and with people who didn't understand what we were doing. Renato and the Catholic Church supported us and helped us organize.

Thank God, we finally won the rights to our land.

Later, we tried to help with another occupation. But they shot a friend of ours, captured others, and finally many policemen and gunmen took over the area. We felt such pain when this failed! We spent our last cent and all of our energy, and they burned down all the houses. We cried and cried!

This very situation of injustice called me to the struggle.

Injustice that some people don't work, but have everything in life, while many people work all day, every day and have *nothing*. Injustice that there are no rich people in prison, but only poor people. The rich steal from the poor, and the one who is stolen from ends up in prison!

ॐ ॐ ॐ

Here in the south of our state of Pará we have a big collision around the meaning of faith. Our rural workers are being massacred by capitalism and the large landowners. As a church, we can't be silent before these injustices!

We're a church of the people and the people need to have life to be a church. So, the church must defend the people.

And the church must continue giving space to the laity.

Before, only priests or nuns would be involved. At this stage of liberation theology the lay people have to make their *own* history. You see, a priest is here for five years and then moves on. But the lay person stays here, involved in the movements, the unions, etc. The struggle goes on even when the priest leaves!

The church isn't only a mission of saying Mass, but a mission of struggling for life, creating history, recovering the true history the people don't yet know.

For example, people still believe that Brazil was all jungle when it was "discovered" by Europeans. This is a lie! We must seek out the true history of the Brazilian people, going back to our roots in the Indians who already lived here and the blacks who were brought here as slaves.

The church also arrived here with the sword! We have to learn our history and correct these faults in the church.

૪ৈ ૪ৈ ૪ৈ

My life wouldn't have meaning if I wasn't in the struggle. The struggle is the battle for our rights, the battle for life. We struggle for that which we deserve but are denied—health care, housing, work.

Faith sustains me in this struggle—the example of Christ the Liberator, who taught us how to struggle for life. Without faith, all my works would be meaningless!

I'm motivated by a certain mysticism. An interior force shakes me up deeply before the bad things happening in our world. Many people don't feel this way.

When I'm discouraged I look to Christ, the source of my strength.

The Bible is so important for us! It gives us courage. Prayer is also very important—it strengthens the spirit! But, we can't leave aside action. Our word for prayer is *oraçao*—which means *ora* [to pray] and *açāo* [action].

Prayers alone don't help. You have to pray and participate.

I really believe that God listens to our prayers. But we can't wait for answers to fall from the heavens! We have to pray to God, believing God will hear, but we have to do something too. If we don't, things will never change.

I believe what Gandhi wrote: those who say religion doesn't have anything to do with politics don't understand religion.

Faith and politics essentially go together.

I don't mean political parties. I mean, every time you take to the streets to demand water, housing, health care—this is politics.

The very Bible contains politics! Jesus denounced the great injustices of the powerful people of his time and defended the little people. Because of this, the powerful people of his time crucified him! The Bible isn't just about the past. It's happening now—Pharaoh isn't that different from our large landowners!

Now, you have to interpret the Bible—if you don't, you'll use the Bible like the evangelical fundamentalists. They use the Bible only for private prayer, but they don't see the action that's implicit in it.

For us, Scripture is like a light that illuminates our journey. But if you just sit and stare at the light, you'll ruin your eyesight!

ॐ ॐ ॐ

I don't want to condemn people who don't have faith, who aren't committed to the struggle. Nothing like this! I'd just like people to pay attention to their own journey, step by step. It's through their own life struggles that they'll find the true motivation and desire to engage in the struggle to transform society.

I hope these people begin to read a chapter, even a verse of the Bible and begin to compare it with what's going on in their lives and in society.

But they have to really stop and reflect—they have to leave aside the comfortable apathy that muddles the struggle a lot these days. Only faith will give them the courage they need!

I believe it's impossible for someone to have a conversion to God without having a conversion to the poor.

God preached liberation for the poor, so ours is a God of the poor and oppressed. It's impossible to talk about God without taking the side of the poor.

But we know that the rich aren't liberated either. They are often slaves to money, ambition, power. And their money makes them slaves to fear. Equality for all people is liberation from fear!

ॐ ॐ ॐ

It is sad to see that here, in the state of Pará, things get more serious every day.

Our rivers are dying—they are polluted from the mercury used by the gold miners panning for gold. Then the people who eat the fish or the animals who drink the poisoned water get sick.

And our forests are disappearing! When I was born the main wealth of our state was rubber. People immigrated here from all over Brazil to extract our rubber. Today, you can hardly find a single rubber tree!

After rubber, our wealth was the *castanha do Pará* [literally the "Pará nut tree," known as the Brazil nut]. But then came the sawmills and men with great ambitions. Today, the Brazil nut tree is nearly extinct!

Millions and millions of trees are cut every day and thrown in the ovens for charcoal, to keep the ironworks running. As if this deforestation weren't enough, the *ashes* from the production of charcoal infects our lungs! At night we can't breathe. The children have asthma, bronchitis, throat diseases—all because of the smoke!

Last year, our neighborhood put up a big struggle against the production of charcoal ovens. A large group of us went to the Secretary of Health who eventually demanded that the ovens be closed. This was a great victory! But many other neighborhoods haven't achieved this.

Listen, the people who work at the ovens know it's awful, but they depend on their meager work to bring daily bread to their children! They know it may kill them in fifteen years, but they have no alternatives.

On top of this, all of these people were once farmers! They sold their lands because the government doesn't give any incentives to small rural workers. It's easier for them to sell their land and make charcoal than to stay there waiting for the beans to grow, without money to buy medicine or shoes for their children, suffering from malaria as well.

This is life for the people of Pará. We didn't know how to protect the trees, and now that we're waking up, there are hardly any trees left! This great threat to life is only going to be combatted when people become aware. We can still save nature—which is life.

Following pages: The local people of Pará call this stretch of deforested land the "cemetery of the Brazil nut tree."

I have a great hope that with the leaven of faith, this mass of converted people will grow and grow. A small majority will come together to transform society.

Yes, we do believe the dance will change!

🎜 🎜 🎜

*How does your Christian faith shape your understanding of the great ecological devastation that is occurring in Pará?*

Our religion is about the living God, the God of life who helps us struggle for life—and ecology is life! I'm a follower of Jesus Christ who valued life above all else—and in the ecological movement, I'm defending life! Look, if they keep up this destruction, then in thirty years Marabá will be a complete desert, with polluted rivers and inedible fish. This is life? This isn't life!

*Toinha, you've helped start women's groups in two neighborhoods. What are the specific problems facing women here?*

We're still living in a very *machista* society. In addition to the discrimination a woman suffers in society, she also has to put up with the burdens of her partner who arrives home exhausted because he was oppressed by his boss. He isn't satisfied with his salary or working hours, but since he can't vent with his boss, he comes home and takes it all out on his wife.

Women also suffer as mothers, who still spend much more time in the house with children than men. It's rare that you'll hear a child say, "Dad, I need a notebook. I'm hungry." They tell the mother. Then the husband comes home angry yelling, "Woman, what do you have to eat? What did you do with the money I gave you? Take the child to the doctor!" The doctor won't see the child because they have no money, then the husband is angry because the mother didn't get the child cured.

And then she has to take care of the house. Very few Brazilian men learn how to share domestic chores or care for a house.

*Do you see much violence against women?*

Yes. Everyone wants to boss women around. If she's married, the husband feels like her owner, not her husband. "It's *my* woman. I'm the boss!" It's also not rare that husbands beat their wives. Or else, when a husband leaves his wife and hears she's going out with other men, he'll even kill her or them. This just happened to a woman down the street who remarried—the husband hired someone to kill her!

There's also a lot of police violence against women. It's not rare that you hear a report on the radio about the police raping and abusing women here in Marabá.

*What do you hope for in your own life as a woman?*

It's difficult to talk about myself personally. Throughout my life, ever since I had self-awareness as a woman, I've dedicated myself to the struggle for human rights, for life, for health care and housing, for true independence.

I also have my fears, though, because people treat women in the struggle like they don't think about getting married or having a house. As a woman, this is confusing for me. Anyway, I think I've advanced beyond the men we have in Brazil!

Still, I'd like to have a companion beside me, but not just anyone. I want someone capable of respecting my limits just as I respect his. A companion who knows how to share domestic chores. I don't want a "master" lording over me. I want a companion to walk side by side with me.

Living alone, I manage to divide my time pretty well among domestic chores, caring for my adopted daughter, spending time with my mother and siblings, and time for the movement, for work, and for studies. I manage all this quite well!

*What is the role of men in this movement of liberation?*

Once men become aware that women are human beings equal to men, things will be much better because men will have the opportunity to be more human, to not be only *machista* men that don't have feelings, that don't cry. Men also need to learn that they will win over women with love and tenderness, not possessiveness.

But they first have to learn to accept women's rights. Men have to stop thinking that women are objects to be possessed and walk with them as companions, side by side. I always say at meetings, "Until men learn to see women as true companions and not competitors for rights, we can't say we have a transformed society." No way.

*What are the biggest problems confronting the church at the base?*

The church today is divided into two blocks—the conservative block and the progressive block or renewed church. As incredible as it sounds, the masses of people are still accustomed to the old church that only said, "Go in peace, God be with you," but didn't do anything for the people.

Our church in Pará is of the progressive block. We're building CEBs and discussing the problems that the people feel in their skin—hunger, sickness, misery, the crimes of the large landowners against the rural workers. The bourgeois church comes down on this church, calling it communist. This is a problem for us.

*Is it possible for rich people to be committed to the struggle for social change?*

I don't count out the possibility, but I think it would be very difficult. I believe the phrase, "There is no wealth that doesn't come from exploitation." So, if a rich person wants to work building the reign of God, he'll naturally stop being rich, because he'll cease to exploit. And if he already exploited people, he'll naturally return the fruits of his exploitation.

If a rich person practices the Gospel, everything will be alright.

*You say that it is impossible for a person to have a conversion to God without having a conversion to the poor. Explain why.*

It's impossible for someone to have a conversion to God without having a conversion to the poor, if we understand conversion as a change of life.

The history of God is the history of a poor people. We see this in the Bible, where God sends the prophets and then his own Son because God's people were being oppressed. Christ even said, "The sick are in need of the doctor, not the healthy." So, those in need of liberation are the oppressed, not those who are already liberated.

But, we know that the majority of the rich aren't exactly liberated either. They are slaves to money, ambition and power.

Their money makes them slaves to fear, fear of change because they fear that they, too, will have to live in misery. They sleep worrying about their company earning or losing money. Beyond this, they think they'll lose all of their friends if they go down in social class.

The more people own, the more enslaved they are.

*So how would a rich person become liberated?*

I believe that with the liberation of the poor, the rich person will lose his or her fear. We have to convince the rich that we're struggling for liberation, not for the misery of the rich. We don't want to see rich people begging in the streets! We want a life of dignity and equality—for the rich person to have his or her house, but that we also have a house. In a truly just society with truly human values, no one needs to be afraid! Equality for all people—this is liberation from fear!

*Do you think that the rich need their consciousness raised to the reality of injustice just as the poor do?*

Yes, and transformation begins in education. The Brazilian way of education is this: "I educate the poor child to serve and the rich child to give orders."

We have to teach our children that respecting life and human rights is the most important thing, that exploitation is the root of human misery. We have to stop teaching our children that the boss is always benevolent and the employee has to do all the work. This is the role of education and catechetics—in a rich or poor neighborhood!

*Do you see the materialistic values of the elites invading the world of the poor?*

Exactly. The system organizes things so that poor persons have the mind of the rich. They think it's foolish to struggle for their rights because the culture of the rich enters their homes through TV and magazines and contaminates the spirit of our people. There are people who will work a whole month to buy an outfit like a rich person wears! We must educate *against* this, educate with alternative values.

*How can people outside Brazil be in solidarity with the people of Brazil?*

Outside of Brazil, you all think Brazil is the country of Carnival, peace, and bounty. But, when the truth is written or told, you see our country is none of this. Brazil is hunger, violence, misery!

Here inside of Brazil, people are scared to death of making this information known because they can be killed. The government doesn't like it when these things are revealed because it affects their image abroad. Publishing this information about our reality and the exchange of information is very important.

*Is there any other message you want to share with people outside of Brazil?*

My message comes from me as an activist and a member of this suffering, marginalized, massacred people in Brazil and Latin America. My message is this: that your government and your own people respect our liberty.

We have a huge foreign debt with the first world. And Brazil signed a new agreement for $2 billion more in loans. We know that this will be paid by the suffering people of Brazil. We are tired of being the object of someone else's profit. We need the help of people in other countries.

It also gives us strength and encouragement to know that you are struggling for the liberation of your own country!

I also ask people to believe in this living God, the God of life and liberation.

The church in Latin America isn't an utopia, but we believe in life and love, the secret of the Gospel. It doesn't matter if you can read or not, if you have a doctorate or not. Here we have communities and illiterate people who are true leaders, sometimes better than people with diplomas!

I also want to tell people, lay people in particular, that we create our own history. The laity have to assume our commitment with the church, the church of the people, walking with the poor. We can't stand around waiting for someone with ten or fifteen degrees to come and do history for us! History is ours.

# 6

# LORI ALTMANN

I support a "silent mission" to the Indigenous. We sinned so much in bringing sickness, death, robbery of land and cultural destruction that we don't have a "good news" to share.

The only way to be redeemed from this historical sin is silence before the Indians. We need to place ourselves beside them without expecting any profit—even the profit of converted souls.

*Lori Altmann was born in the interior of the state of Rio Grande do Sul, in southern Brazil, where her parents were farmers. Raised a Lutheran, she participated in Lutheran youth groups and was very active in student groups in the sixties, during the years of repression. Lori was ordained a Lutheran pastor and married her husband, also a Lutheran pastor, in 1978. They lived for seven years with the Kulina Indigenous people in the remote Amazon.*

*Today Lori is studying sociology of religion in São Paulo and continues to be an advocate for the rights of Indigenous peoples in Brazil.*

*Drawing often on the teachings of Bishop Pedro Casaldáliga, Lori believes in "silent evangelization"—repenting for the Christian church's complicity in five hundred years of genocide. In the sixteenth century, five million indigenous lived in Brazil. Only 230,000 remain today. 1992 marked the celebration of 500 years*

Lori Altmann stands on the balcony of her high-rise São Paulo apartment. Her T-shirt carries a quote from a Kaingáng Indigenous woman: "Today our cry is a sad lament, from a race that was once happy, because in the past every day was the day of the Indian."

*of Christian evangelization in the Americas. For Lori Altmann, as for Casaldáliga, the Quincentennary was a time of mourning and repentance instead of celebration.*

*Several people in the São Paulo area recommended that I meet Lori Altmann because of her courage, convictions and commitments—especially her dedication to the Indigenous people of Brazil. I met Lori on my last day in Brazil, weaving my way to her high-rise São Paulo apartment on a rainy day. I waited an hour with her two older children until Lori returned from the doctor with her very sick eight month old infant. We visited after lunch, as Lori breastfed her child. During the interview, the faces of Indigenous children, women and men, looked at us from posters and photographs on the walls of her study.*

🍂 🍂 🍂

When I was young, I was very involved with the Lutheran youth movement and eventually participated at the national level.

This motivated me to study theology, though it was rare for women to study theology then. I would have done this earlier if there hadn't been such strong opposition—my family, my pastor and my own community thought that theology and ministry weren't appropriate roles for women!

🍂 🍂 🍂

My social commitment was formed by the university students' movement.

The students were the first ones with the courage to take to the streets and confront the military dictatorship in the sixties and seventies.

In the sixties, there was also a push to do more contextualized theology, within the concrete reality of Brazil. We wanted a theology that was more committed with the grassroots struggles. We formed our own small groups to discuss liberation theology, which wasn't yet a part of the curriculum.

You see, there were very few opportunities for this kind of pastoral practice because of the origins of the Lutheran church.

Lori breastfeeding her infant.

It was culturally very Germanic, very closed, middle class, and quite conservative.

Next we started a group for people interested in the Indigenous question, working with the Jesuits of São Leopoldo. During our theology course we were required to do an eight month internship, and I asked to work in the diocese of Dom Pedro Casaldáliga.

In 1978, my husband and I spent a year with the Indigenous people, but we were expelled by FUNAI ( *Fundaão Nacional do Indio*—the National Foundation of the Indian), the government agency that oversees work with the Indigenous. We began our work again in 1980, spending seven years with the Kulina people in the remote Amazon.

Our first goal with the Indigenous was complete immersion in their way of life. Complete adaptation to their culture, language and world-view.

Then, from within, we sought to accompany them in their concrete daily struggles—land issues, community organization, economic struggles. We worked in the fields with them, and my second child was born in the village according to tribal customs.

Later, we saw that while insertion was an important phase, it wasn't sufficient. We had to break the isolation. So we moved into the work of accompaniment and advisory assistance. We began to reach out to other villages, meet with other tribes and form alliances with rubber-tappers and outside groups.

We also began literacy classes—in their language, using texts they created, learning their stories and myths, studying their reality. We always linked language and literacy with the information and other tools necessary for the struggle. We eventually began training monitors from each village to learn from each other and work together to demand their rights.

ఞ ఞ ఞ

Living with the Indigenous really has influenced my spirituality.

Contact with them called into question our faith and theology, even central theological points. Ultimately, it strengthened my faith, but I was compelled to re-read my faith with a new lens.

For example, Lutheran theology was always centered in the question of sin and grace. The language of Indigenous groups didn't even have the concept of sin!

Then I understood that all of these Lutheran conflicts, sin and justification, which may have been important for Luther's era, had nothing to do with these people.

Sin is not theirs, but ours as white people!

Ours is a historical sin, starting the moment we invaded this continent. As Christians, we supported the process of colonization and occupation of this land and these peoples.

So, it wasn't a matter of us teaching the Indians about sin and justification through Christ. This isn't framed right! We don't need to discover where sin is among them, but where it is among *us*—as Christians, as whites on an Indigenous continent.

I support a "silent mission."

We sinned so much in bringing sickness, death, robbery of land and cultural destruction that we have little "good news" to share. The original meaning of evangelization is "good news." But, this Christian message arrived as *bad* news, accompanied by death and domination.

To be redeemed from this historical sin, we must be *silent* before the Indians. We need to place ourselves beside them without expecting any profit—even the profit of converts. This is the penitential silence Pedro Casaldáliga talks about.

ᏸ ᏸ ᏸ

Our children actually aided our work with the Indigenous. They helped us become integrated in the community.

Since I left there, I've always felt the difficulties having children—especially with academic life. Our society really separates the world of adults and children. São Paulo offers day care and nurseries and schools, but all of these alternatives separate the child from the family!

In the village, if there was a meeting, everyone came—women, children, men. These meetings were in the middle of the village and, as the houses had no walls in the kitchen, the women could participate and share opinions from the fireside. It was a much more relaxed, communitarian and integrated life.

When my second child was born, I breastfed other children when I had too much milk, just as other women helped feed him. There was always mutual aid there, not just one married couple alone like in our society.

In the city, I'm made to feel ashamed of being a mother. As if breastfeeding were a diminishment of women!

ॐ ॐ ॐ

I believe that spirituality is very important, especially in times of discouragement and frustration such as the church and society are experiencing in Brazil today.

Speaking as a Lutheran, we reacted against an alienating spirituality that was in the heavens but not on earth. From there we entered into activism. But many people didn't take time to stop and focus on finding another kind of spirituality.

Spirituality gives us the energy to face difficulties.

The road is very far, and maybe people don't see any results.

If we don't have a constant celebration, if we don't know how to have spaces of liberty and happiness inside of the very struggle, inside of our very journey, then we won't have the energy to continue our struggle to the very end.

ॐ ॐ ॐ

*What have you learned from the Indigenous about the ecological crisis?*

The Indigenous people have a much more integrated vision of the world than we do. Their very survival depends on the conservation of nature. Add to this that they're very dispersed populations, with few people, and they don't work under the notion of accumulation. They work for necessity, for use.

The desire for accumulation really provokes the destruction of nature. For example, the big landowner destroys a large part of the jungle because he desires profits, whereas when the Indians gather fruit, they spread the seeds that guarantee the growth of new trees. This should be an example to us all!

"I heard the cry of my Indigenous people." Poster in Lori's study.

# OUVI O CLAMOR DO MEU POVO INDÍGENA

**COMIN**-CONSELHO DE MISSÃO ENTRE ÍNDIOS
**CEM**-CENTRO DE ELABORAÇÃO DE MATERIAL
**DEPARTAMENTO DE CATEQUESE**
**GRUPO MARÇAL TUPÃ I**
**CONAJE**- CONSELHO NACIONAL DA JUVENTUDE
EVANGÉLICA
**GTME**-GRUPO DE TRABALHO MISSIONÁRIO EVANGÉLICO
**CONSELHO DO PROJETO MISSÃO ENTRE OS POVOS CINTA LARGA, ZORÓ E SURUÍ (RO)**

**CAPA-RE III**-CENTRO DE ACONSELHAMENTO AO PEQUENO
AGRICULTOR
**CAPA-RE IV**-CENTRO DE APOIO AO PEQUENO AGRICULTOR
**PPL**-PASTORAL POPULAR LUTERANA
**EST**-ESCOLA SUPERIOR DE TEOLOGIA
**COREMIN-RE II**-CONSELHO REG. DE MISSÃO ENTRE ÍNDIOS
**DE YUCUMÃ**-GRUPO DE APOIO À MISSÃO ENTRE ÍNDIOS

**1990**

KARIN ROSENBAUM

*How has liberation theology responded to the struggles of the Indigenous?*

There's a really strong pastoral practice with the Indigenous inside the church, especially the Catholic church. But, there's no theoretical elaboration. Liberation theology is still fixed on social class, which has eclipsed the ethnic dimension.

But maybe this reflection won't come from Brazil, because we don't have a Indigenous pastoral project but an "Indigenist" one. A truly Indigenous pastoral project would be done by the Indigenous themselves. The "Indigenist" project is done *by* the whites *for* the Indians. This isn't always the case in Bolivia, Peru, Ecuador, where the majority of the population is Indigenous. There the Indigenous *are* the theologians, pastors, priests. Maybe from these places a truly Indigenous theology will arise— a reflection in the perspective of liberation theology, but with Indigenous historical and cultural roots.

*Where else do you think liberation theology needs to grow?*

Well, the only way liberation theology can grow is if we do away with some of the centralism in the Catholic church. The difficulty I see is that the CEBs reach a certain point of democratization and then hit a limit—the priest, the bishop, the Pope. Because of this, many community leaders are leaving pastoral work to get involved in other movements, political parties, etc. There needs to be a change allowing married priests, women's ordination—a *democratization* of leadership overall.

*As an ordained Lutheran minister, do you feel that as a woman you have more space to excercise leadership than your Catholic colleagues do?*

Well, in legal and theological terms, we have more space than Catholics. According to Lutheran theology, through baptism we are called to the universal priesthood of believers. And as women, we've reached the "last" space—ordination.

That doesn't mean we women don't have difficulties! We still have very few women pastors—forty out of eight hundred! And women still encounter resistance and discrimination from communities and colleagues, even other pastors. The patriarchal mentality is very entrenched.

*What differences do you notice in the theology being elaborated by women in the First World and women in Latin America?*

First World feminist theologians have been working much longer at theoretical development. But their theology isn't enough for me because it lacks the mark of social class, a characteristic of the Third World. Their theology may relate very well to their environment, but we have to consider the issue of the poor woman. We can't speak about women in general in Latin America. We have to make a class distinction.

We also have very few theologians at the doctoral level. We may already have a reflection, but we're so involved at the base that we often don't have the time or means to sit down and formulate this theoretically. We ask the women theologians in the North to respect our pastoral practice, just as we respect their theological production.

We need a dialogue where we can both learn from each other.

*What has your life experience with the Indigenous communities taught you about the meaning of the option for the poor?*

Well, we used to believe that the option for the poor meant becoming poor among the poor. This meant a sacrifice of money and comforts—a lower salary and less possessions. We tried to not use airplanes because the poor couldn't afford it. We'd use the bus instead. Things like that.

But we've matured from this and recognized that our big sacrifices, in political terms, didn't always help! It didn't help change things for the poor. Living with the Indigenous we learned that more important than becoming poor was the effort to really open ourselves, trying to understand their culture and lifestyle.

We also came to learn that to be in solidarity with the poor we didn't have to give up everything or stop being who we were. I'll always be middle class, even if I lower my salary. We're middle class by the very way we understand society, our level of education, our access to persons and power. We can't deny our own history!

But, we do have to place our gifts and our work at the service of changing society. We have to use our goods to serve the grassroots struggle.

*If in women's liberation men lose privilege but also gain their own liberation, do the rich also gain liberation as well as losing privilege as the poor become liberated?*

Certainly, the wealth of the rich is a consequence of the poverty of the poor. This is obvious when some have so much and others have less than they should. But I don't think rich people are bad. This is a poor judgment. There's a sinful system that sacrifices the rich as much as the poor. Clearly there's a difference—the rich suffer from full stomachs and the poor suffer from empty stomachs.

I don't know, it seems that in the U.S. and Europe there's a loss of meaning—people have everything, but they don't have a dream! They don't have anything to hope for! In this sense, I think they're extremely anguished because, in clinging to their wealth, they become extremely isolated. They protect themselves from others to preserve what they possess.

So, the lessening of differences between the rich and poor will benefit the poor as well as the rich, in different ways.

*How can people in the First World be in solidarity with the people of Brazil?*

International solidarity is very important for issues like the Indigenous and ecology. Foreigners can denounce and pressure our government and international organizations like the World Bank, which funds destructive projects in Brazil.

For example, the greatest suffering of the poor in all Latin America is from the payment of the foreign debt. We need international pressure, like the movements against U.S. intervention in Central America. We need this for all of the Third World.

Many people are also concerned with changing their lifestyle to respect the environment. Our lifestyle choices are a testimony that gradually build an alternative system to consumerism and profit. In the long run, this will also trigger results.

*What message would you like to share with people in the U.S.?*

My message to people there, especially the women, is that they maintain their critical spirit towards this system that brings benefits to them, but at the cost of the suffering of the poor in Latin America and all over the world.

I realize that women in the U.S. also face much discrimination, especially Hispanics, African Americans and Native Americans. They suffer double for being women and poor. Here in Brazil poverty is more widespread; it seems it's easier there to hide poverty, so it's almost not seen.

# 7

# FREI BETTO

A spirituality of liberation is grounded in an *affective* relationship with God and with the people.

It's not enough to have the bonds of *effective* work with the communities. I must make the community members my friends—drink beer and play soccer with them.

I can't merely be a vending machine of faith!

*Frei ("Brother") Betto was born in 1944, the second of eight children in a well-off family. As a teenager, Frei Betto was active with Catholic Action[†]; by the age of fifteen, he led the student movement of his city, Belo Horizonte; and at seventeen, he was national director of the Young Catholic Students movement. At twenty-one he became a Dominican brother and was imprisoned at the age of twenty-five for five years because of his work helping dissidents escape the country.*

*Based in the city of São Paulo, Frei Betto is known internationally for his prolific writings, especially* Against Principalities

---

[†]Catholic Action, a movement of lay persons founded in Belgium in the late twenties, was important in Brazil until the 1964 –1968 counter-revolution. Through its many branches—Young Workers, Students, Intellectuals, etc.—it helped people to become aware of structural injustice. Many members were imprisoned by the military because of their actions in favor of the poor. It was one of the factors that helped to "open" the Church, leading to Vatican II and, in Latin America, to Medellín.

Many of the members of Students' Catholic Action helped to found Popular Action in the early sixties. Their aim was to empower the poor. As it gradually became more radical, its members were often persecuted, imprisoned and tortured by the military.

*and Powers: Letters From a Brazilian Jail (1971), and his book of interviews with Fidel Castro, Fidel and Religion (1987). He currently works with the Labor Pastoral Project in Brazil's principal industrial city, São Bernardo do Campo, outside of São Paulo. He also assists the popular movements, the CEBs, and promotes grassroots education. He recently published a novel on street children in Brazil.*

*In 1993, Frei Betto was sued by the São Paulo Secretary of Public Safety and the high command of the São Paulo Military Police for defaming the military. The conflict was sparked by a newspaper article he wrote condemning police violence aimed at children who are black and poor. Frei Betto was acquitted early in July of 1993; later that month eight homeless young boys were gunned down in Rio de Janeiro. Three human rights groups in Brazil documented more than 4,500 extra judicial executions of children and adolescents between 1988 and 1990. The same trend continues today.*

*I met Frei Betto at his monastery residence near downtown São Paulo. As we talked, his packed bags in the doorway reminded me of how little time we had before his late evening journey to attend out-of-town meetings.*

*Frei Betto tells me his heroes are Jesus, the mystics Teresa of Avila and St. John of the Cross, the revolutionary Ché Guevarra, Lula (the Brazilian socialist and union leader who nearly became president), and mystic-philosopher Simone Weil. He also makes me promise to use the name "Frei Betto" instead of his official name "Carlos Alberto Libanio Christo."*

ﷺ ﷺ ﷺ

My mother was an activist Christian with a very open mind. She really shaped me. My father was very anti-clerical, probably because of his rigid Christian upbringing. When he found out that I entered the monastery, he cried as if it were a funeral! Then he didn't speak to me for a year.

During the sixties, when Brazil was under the military, my stance became more revolutionary. Catholic Action gave me a Christianity that was very linked to social justice. And I was also very influenced by France's "social Catholicism".

A view of downtown São Paulo.

I then became a collaborator with a movement of Christian revolutionaries in Brazil called Popular Action. As collaborators, some other Dominicans and I worked with persecuted students, helping them leave the country. The military arrested me and charged me with subversion against the government.

I was held twenty-two months before a trial, then sentenced to four more years. While I was in prison, my father changed from being a right-winger to being more progressive and allied with the people.

Two things sustained me in prison—prayer and writing.

Prison became an opportunity to deepen my experience of God. And writing helped me to not be so traumatized—it transformed prison into a literary experience.

ॐ ॐ ॐ

The dominant spirituality of our church puts God on a mountain top.

In this view, we Christians have to scale the mountain by degrees through the practice of moral virtues. We spend our lives like the myth of Sisyphus, trying to carry the rock of virtues. Yet the weight of our sins is very great, and each time we reach a certain height of the mountain, we fall to the bottom, begin again, and fall yet again.

This is a non-liberating spirituality. A liberating spirituality is that of Jesus. Which is? Well, the primary demand is not moral behavior to bring one closer to God. It's the inverse! There is no mountain! Rather, there is a God who pours Godself out in love for all of us.

For me, prayer means letting oneself be loved by God.

I have moments in my daily life when I'm attentive to the embrace of God. My way of prayer, meditation and breathing, allows me to pray on the street, in my work, even at a union meeting.

St. John's letter says God is love. The one who loves knows God. St. John doesn't say that whoever knows God, loves. Whoever loves, with or without faith, lives the experience of God. And there is no one that God doesn't love.

As St. Augustine says, God is more intimate with us that we are with ourselves.

Opening myself to the love of God, in all of my sins, I establish an affective relationship, and from this relationship of love, fidelity is born. A man is faithful to his spouse and she to him, not because there's a law, but because they so love each other that they cannot *not* be faithful.

This is the spirituality Jesus presents: God is Abba, Daddy, someone very intimate who welcomes the prodigal son. The one who sinned the most is the one who deserves the party, because God is always giving.

A spirituality of liberation is grounded in an affective relationship with God and with the people. It is not enough to have the bonds of effective work with the communities. I must make the community members my friends—drink beer and play soccer with them. I can't merely be a vending machine of faith!

ᔎ ᔎ ᔎ

For centuries in Latin America, we announced the word of God from the European perspective. With Vatican II, we felt the challenge of announcing God in a continent where the majority live without the essentials for biological survival.

From there we began to speak about God starting from the poor. And the great aspiration of the poor is to *liberate* themselves from suffering, oppression, sickness, the lack of food and work.

Liberation theology wants to create a society where men and women are free from that which prevents them from being truly human, as much from the material side—work, food, housing, health, school—as from the spiritual side.

As St. Thomas said in the Middle Ages, you can't demand that a starving person practice moral virtues. Minimally, we must first secure someone's biological survival.

A spirituality of liberation is centered on the God of life—a God who is revealed in the communion of love with other persons! This spirituality means that we devote much time to liturgical action and personal prayer—gratuitous prayer.

Gratuity is being present without utility. It's being with God, one or two hours a day, without expecting this time to be effective or productive.

We Western Christians have lost this gratuitous dimension of prayer! It's impeded by our rationalist culture. Too often we speak about God, we speak with God, but we don't let God speak to us. Gratuity is this: letting God speak.

Just as a married couple has moments of intimacy, we need to have moments of intimacy with God.

While this spirituality is Christian, it's universal in the sense that we're all in the universe, the womb of God. One day we will be born.

You see, God is in all people—even those without faith.

Every person who loves has an experience of God. A manager of a store in New York who today is loving, is experiencing God. He doesn't know it, but one day he will!

ᛰᛰ ᛰᛰ ᛰᛰ

*Having worked for years among the grassroots movements, what insights do you bring to liberation theology? What direction would you like to see it go in the future?*

First, liberation theology needs to stress more and more the mystical experience. It also needs to work better with popular religiosity. We're very rationalist, but the people absorb things in their skin, not in abstract concepts. Our ministry should be less discursive and more experiential, more festive, more liturgical!

We must also re-think the proposal of our evangelization for constructing justice in Latin America in light of the failure of the socialist model in Eastern Europe. We have to make two things clear. First, the failure of socialism in Eastern Europe is not the failure of socialism itself. Secondly, capitalism is three hundred years old and has always failed—because for any one successful capitalist country, twenty have failed! For example, all the countries of Latin America are capitalist, but none of them are working! We have to restore the utopia of a new society.

*I read the article in which you call on the grassroots movements of the left to pay more attention to ecological questions, yet you also warn of the ecological movement being co-opted into a bourgeois project.*

There are three angles to the ecological question.

A young boy sleeps on a bench in downtown São Paulo. Frei Betto stood trial (and was acquitted) on the charge of defaming the military in his articles that denounced military police brutality against such children.

The first is based in biblical fundamentalism, which says that God created nature and gave it to men and women to use or abuse. This is the perspective of Exxon, Coca Cola and the cigarette companies that finance ecological campaigns to cover up the utilitarian and manipulative way they lord over nature—polluting, contaminating, etc.—for immediate profits.

The second angle sees nature as a sanctuary. We have to protect the Amazon, our lungs, the whales, the trees, the water. But, what about *the poor* of Africa, Asia, Latin America? This perspective is a naturalism that excludes the human being.

The third angle sees men and women as part of nature. The central figure of this is the rubber-tapper and union leader Chico Mendes, who was murdered by the cattle ranchers in 1988. Not one thing occurs in nature that doesn't affect us, and nothing happens to us that doesn't affect nature. The ecological question cannot, by any means, be unconnected to the issue of justice.

This is what we want in Brazil today. But the ecological banner is in the hands of the Brazilian Right, as if it were something romantic or idyllic. To truly understand ecological issues, we must listen to the *victims* of ecological problems and the people in direct contact with nature—Indians, rubber-tappers, gold miners, the rural workers.

*Does liberation theology have something to offer to this movement?*

We're trying to make a theological reflection on the issue of ecology, precisely within a holistic panorama. We cannot separate the problem of the Amazon from the problem in the Persian Gulf, from the problem of the *favela* in Rio!

The symbol of this planet, the true symbol of peace, has to be a cross. That is, harmony between East and West must be accompanied by a new order between North and South. Until this happens, every regional conflict immediately affects the whole international system.

*What is your understanding of the conflict between the Vatican and the church of liberation in Latin America?*

With the Second Vatican Council we achieved plurality, this richness of charisms in the universal church through the spe-

cific features of each church. The center of the conflict today is
the Vatican project of "uniformizing" the universal church according to the Vatican's neo-colonialist model. Now, I don't believe this imposition will be successful. The Vatican can replace
bishops and even some priests, but they can't replace the people. The faith of the people is very deep-rooted.

Also, the church doesn't have any alternative in Latin America—without the CEBs, the church won't survive! We must evangelize through small communities. Today people have TV and a
series of consumer goods, and the church has become something
nostalgic. The church doesn't matter to them unless they're in-
serted in a community that gives true religious meaning to
liturgy, parties, celebrations.

*Do you think there's a connection between the Vatican and the
secular elites who criticize and harass representatives of the
church of liberation?*

Sure—there's an ideological link! All of these people believe
that the bourgeois project of capitalist society is the best the
world has to offer. At the core, the Vatican has never really believed there's any way but the market economy. It's never radically critiqued bourgeois liberalism—nor has it ever presented an
alternative.

So, these people think that a certain social inequality is in-
herently necessary. They think that the people of the Third World
aren't as rich as Europe because, who knows, they didn't work
hard enough!

*There is much talk these days about the growth of Pentecostal
churches. Being so involved in the CEBs, how do you explain the
booming popularity of Pentecostalism?*

I want to draw attention to two phenomena. Where do sects
flourish? Not in São Paulo, where the CEBs are functioning, but
in Rio, where there are none. This is the same in the interior.

Second, the sects grow because of the utter misery that exists among forty million Brazilians. People in misery need solutions yesterday, not today! People will go to that pastor who
promises healing to a person without any access to medical care.

This isn't a threat to us, because the work of the sects is "immediatist," a religious "clientalism" that serves up immediate solutions. I won't argue with anyone over who has bigger numbers. We want communities that have quality consciousness.

*What can the Catholic church learn from the Pentecostals' rate of growth?*

We can learn from them to democratize our ministries! Our priests spend eight years in formation! Their pastors spend one or two years! This would be difficult for our clerical church. The CEBs are a source of vocations for the church, but we first have to do away with mandatory celibacy and change the formation system.

*Do you think it's possible to form a CEB among the middle-class?*

Many people from the middle- and upper-class have made an option to work with grassroots ministry. The difficulty is in creating base communities specifically of middle- and upper-class people that would go beyond just meetings and reflections.

That is, as long as the meetings work as the level of discourse, fine. But, when you say, "Now, what are we going to do?" then it's like the Gospel story—one has a daughter that's getting married, another has an estate to care for, someone else has a funeral to go to, and so on.

*So what does the option for the poor really mean for any of us?*

This option for the poor is the bread and butter one chooses for one's life. That is, my life project either goes in the direction of strengthening justice for the poor or in the direction of strengthening the oppressive system for the rich minority.

*How can we make solidarity concrete?*

First, Americans can open the windows of their houses a little bit and seek to discover their closest neighbors, the Latin Americans.

Second, the Americans need to understand that much of their well-being is the fruit of our poverty. For centuries, our raw materials and our labor served to enrich the U.S. and Europe. Today the time has arrived for North Americans to return, in solidarity, that which was taken from us by their governments and large companies.

I think we can give Americans, I don't know, maybe that which still remains alive in our society, that's not been totally contaminated by consumerism—our humanity, solidarity, something of happiness. I believe our links with Americans will help many people become much more humanized.

# 8

## SILVIA REGINA DE LIMA SILVA

I think our efforts to speak of a Black God, a Mother God, a Worker God serve to de-mystify what's been passed on to us. The church made God's image so distant from us!

Yet every effort to absolutize an image of God falls to the ground. Here is a God who doesn't have a face—thus a God who can assume *all* faces.

*Silvia Regina is a theology student at the Pontifical University in Rio (known as the "PUC"). A Franciscan sister for ten years, she now lives in a small religious community of Afro-Brazilians, dedicated to serving the black population on the periphery of Rio de Janeiro. Silvia took up theology to inform her pastoral work with the CEBs, but is more and more considering becoming a theologian, continuing in solidarity with the Afro-Brazilian movement and women's groups.*

*I first learned of Silvia Regina de Lima Silva through an article she wrote for Brazil's* Pastoral Life *magazine, titled "The Black Woman and her Challenges: Towards an Afro-American (women's) Theology." Arriving in Rio with no address or phone number for her, I was delighted to discover that she was a student of my Rio host, Tereza Cavalcanti, who graciously arranged a meeting for us.*

*I met Silvia at a bus station in Baixada Fluminese, known internationally as one of Brazil's most violent "slums." Indeed, the*

Silvia campaigns for Benedita da Silva on election day, handing out leaflets for the Workers' Party. Benedita da Silva won the election, becoming Brazil's first black congress woman.

99

*periphery of Rio de Janeiro is plagued by gangs, drug dealing, vig-
ilante executions and police brutality. Silvia's neighborhood is
poor—mud roads, makeshift homes, people struggling for dignity,
safety, survival. Because she chooses to live here, at the periphery, among the poor, she ends up commuting four or five hours
daily to and from Rio for classes.*

*Silvia appeared an hour late, breathless and cheerful after
passing out campaign literature for congressional candidate
Benedita da Silva and the Worker's Party. After the interview in
her community home, Silvia insisted that I stay for cake. She
hastily scrounged together some flour, sugar, eggs and chocolate
powder from the seemingly bare kitchen and served up a delicious
cake, beaming, "We must have communion and break bread with
our new friend!"*

ℬ ℬ ℬ

I'm twenty-eight years old, the youngest of four children.

I was born into a simple family. My father worked with a telephone company. My parents weren't rich, but they always managed to send us to good Catholic schools. We lived in a decent
house with a phone and a car. But the poverty of others upset
me deeply.

One Christmas, when I was eleven or twelve years old, I
didn't want to celebrate with the rest of my family at my grandmother's house. I wanted to stay with the people who lived
under a bridge nearby.

My parents exploded! They were really involved in the community, but they still didn't understand. So, my father convinced
me to go to my grandmother's house, but first we got a bag of food
together and distributed it among the poor.

At fifteen, I chose to enter the Franciscan convent.

I don't know how to explain why, except that I didn't want a
monotonous life. I wanted something different. I loved religious
life and began to work with people in the *favela*. People said, "My!
A fifteen year old nun!" And I made many friends.

> This simple "shrine" in the corner of Silvia's bed-
> room includes a statue of Brazil's patron saint,
> the black Nossa Senhora Aparecida; a flag for
> Lula, the Workers' Party 1989 presidential candi-
> date; a booklet on black women; pan flutes and
> other religious and cultural symbols.

After a while, though, I burned out completely. I wasn't in touch with my own problems. But I continued working in the community and I stayed a Franciscan sister for ten years.

ᵱᵃ ᵱᵃ ᵱᵃ

The strongest moment in my life happened about six years ago, when I discovered my own blackness.

I had a few earlier memories of a growing awareness of being black. My mother was mulatto, fairer skinned, and my father was black. We had frizzy hair so it was always a big *fight* to comb our hair. She said, "Don't cry or it will make your father sad!"

We thought he felt bad that he'd given us this hair!

These memories helped me recover my identity, the identity of my people.

So, six years ago I joined the Black Pastoral Agents.[†] I studied philosophy in a seminary, and we formed a group of black religious. From then on, my other work became problematic because I wanted to focus more on the concerns of blacks.

This was the most decisive moment of my life.

I loved the Franciscans and felt deep affection for the women. But I began to see that I couldn't carry on both works—the congregation and the cause of the black people.

I had to choose.

I chose to continue religious life, but completely dedicated to working with the black people. That's how we formed our own community, the Black Missionary Community.

I came to this neighborhood, Baixada Fluminese, on the periphery of Rio, with the hope of seeing a new form of religious commitment emerge.

It was difficult, but I really believe in religious movements that arise from the communities and neighborhoods themselves—creating their own forms of religious life and ordained ministry.

Today we are three people in my community—myself, Jose and Geraldio—with a specific ministry to the black people. We

---

[†]A group of black priests, seminarians, sisters and lay persons who experience a deep link between their faith and the consciousness of their blackness, helping other black people to become aware of their dignity. They are an ecumenical group, though often linked with the Catholic church.

make the same vows of celibacy, poverty and obedience and are linked with the diocesan bishop who welcomed us here, Dom Mauro Morelli.

Looking at the history of the church and religious congregations in Brazil, we see there was *never* anything like this—a special ministry to care for the black people!

This very motivation brought our community to life.

⚜ ⚜ ⚜

We live a very harsh reality in our neighborhood.

Baixada Fluminese is filled with violence, disrespect and injustice. *Physical* violence, police violence, death squads who are killing off whole families! Death itself.

The black people are the greatest victims of this! And men are the greater victims, though I've seen more and more women raped and killed by death squads.

These things don't just happen by chance. It's a very well planned-out, organized injustice.

As a church, we're still a weak voice amidst all the violence. But this situation of constantly facing death demands more of us. More courage. I believe that the God we profess is a God who demands that we get more involved with this reality.

I am worried lately about the ever growing distance between the church and the communities—a separation that comes from the hierarchy, not from the communities!

I'm also worried about some of my friends—good people, partners in the struggle—who are beginning to feel threatened by this conflict.

You see, opting for the poor, opting for the communities, for the black people, for women means the punishment of losing space before the traditional, hierarchical church. Losing your job, for example.

You see, the communities are becoming a place of a different kind of power than the power the traditional church has always held. And the Vatican perceives this! It sees the journey of the Latin American church and recognizes that Rome isn't the center of the world! God is revealed in other places!

This is a displacement. The presence and revelation of the Spirit don't have a fixed place! The Spirit blows where it will—not just in the magisterium, but in the midst of the people! This is the source of much conflict.

So, many people committed to this project are turning back, afraid of losing the little power they have.

In this moment, I believe that each one of us is called to carry our option to its ultimate consequences. We're trying to do this in our community. And we're going to see it through.

ॐ ॐ ॐ

Reflecting on the situation of women in our neighborhood has prompted me to begin writing about Mary. You see, the image of Mary was used to justify the situation we women found ourselves in—submission, silence, the negation of life.

That is, Mary as a woman who is white, virgin and mother, serene, delicate, straight and long hair, blue eyes, thin lips, a pious look on her face, young, slender, a halo on her head, with a white baby in her arms, submissive, who always says "yes"— never says "no."

What identification can she have with black women—with the Marias and Creuzas and Monicas of our people?

Black women, prostituted and raped by life, pregnant with children, with faces that are tired, long-suffering, beaten down, sweating, losing teeth, frizzy hair, with glasses, carrying fruit or sweets to sell, thick lips, a flat nose, many with a body already showing the years of her life.

Where's the identification?

For us black women, the church's image of Mary is a negation of our very way of being, a negation of our body. We've heard about Mary as the one who always said "Yes," who always did the will of God. But the "will of God" in the concrete life of the church and the people means that a man gives orders!

I can give you many examples from our neighborhood!

A woman whose husband drinks a lot told her mother-in-law, "When we have relations, I feel hatred because I'm not with his person, but with his drinking."

And the mother-in-law answered, "My child, when you married him you said, 'yes,' and this is for times of happiness and sadness, health and sickness. You should be there to serve your husband." And Mary is invoked as the one who always said "Yes!"

This is completely out of place and manipulated!

But it's very much in the heads of the people. For instance, when you try to gather women together to talk about this situation, it's very difficult because this image of Mary has been with them since childhood.

*We* are the ones who have perpetuated this image! We have to pass on a new image to our daughters.

Today we're trying to read Mary anew.

We discover that Mary's "yes" is given to God's plan of love, salvation and liberation.

The very Canticle of Mary, the Magnificat, recovers the words of the Old Testament, professing faith in a God who's on the side of the people, the God of the poor. Yahweh, who is present in the affliction of the people, present in the struggle, present in the flight out of Egypt. God, who makes a covenant with the people.

Mary is a woman who is present and committed to the historical moment that she lives! We're trying to recover this image of women.

It is really important for us to be present and committed to our moment in history! Women today have to respond "yes" to the pleas of our time.

I wrote a piece called "Mary, the Woman who Said No."

You see, her "yes" brings a series of "no's"—to every situation of exploitation and injustice. Here in our neighborhood, you also have to be a woman who says "No!"

ॐ ॐ ॐ

The two most important forces in my life are God who becomes incarnate and God who escapes all our definitions.

The incarnation is the most beautiful thing that can happen! God so much wants to be committed to the human person that God becomes human; enters what is most deeply human.

Yet every effort to put God into codes, norms, creeds and dogmas falls short. God is beyond all that. This stirs me to always be looking for God.

I will never grasp the mystery of God!

We must remember that society, the church, and even families structure themselves very much on the image of God they hold.

We were taught "God the Father." But for us women, our experience of God was much more of a Mother—in God's closeness, tenderness, friendship. We experience God as Trinity, as Community who unites all kinds of possibilities and diversities!

So we speak of a Black God, Mother God, Worker God.

This de-mystifies what's been passed on to us! In our process of organization and liberation of our people, it's important to meet a God who is more like us.

Yet God throws down every effort to absolutize God.

God is dynamic—diversity, unity, communion. Here is a God who doesn't have a face—thus a God who can assume all faces.

I think God is disconcerting. God escapes us.

The fullness of God unites masculine, feminine, all peoples, all races.

ঞ ঞ ঞ

*How would you describe the situation of blacks in Brazil today?*

You notice today, when you went from Rio to Baixada Fluminese, that as the number of blacks increase, the conditions get worse. We feel this great difference.

The pretense is that Brazil is a racial democracy! But we feel racial discrimination that is both subtle and schematic. In the work place the lowest paying, most arduous jobs are done by the black population. Even when blacks and whites have the same position and the same training, they still receive different salaries. And certain criteria are listed for some jobs—for example, in Brazil they talk a lot about "good appearances," which really means "blacks need not apply."

All of us are victims, especially women.

The same with education. In our region, a great number of our school age children don't go to school because there are so few public schools here. We even suffer discrimination in the very content of our school books! Look at the images and stories passed on to the black people! Where is the history of our people? Our heroes? Our struggles? These are practically unknown!

Brazil has the second largest black population in the world! When will we have access to the history of Africa instead of just Portugal and Spain? A people without a history, without memory, without heroes is a people who is easily manipulated.

The black population also suffers politically. The parties manipulate blacks. They'll put a black person on their ballot, but they don't have real consciousness of racial issues. Even the Left focuses on class, putting racial and cultural issues in second place. But these are weighty issues with us! We are poor and

Silvia sits on her bed in a room decorated with posters celebrating women and blacks.

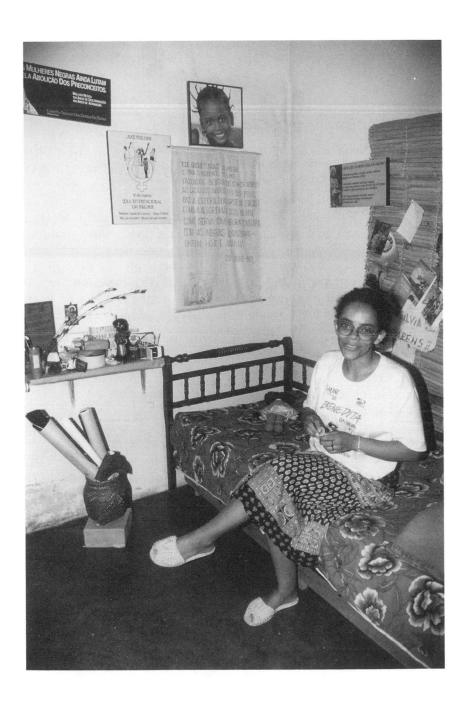

black, we are black and poor. These are profoundly linked! We will only overcome our poverty when we deal with these together.

*Are you familiar with black theologians in the U.S.? How does your work differ from theirs?*

I know a little bit about the black movement in the U.S. I think North American blacks have managed to penetrate the system, to climb the ladder of positions and possessions. But they don't critique the very system.

For us, it's necessary to change the very system so that blacks can even have a place. By no means do we want to make a pact with this system! Along with other grassroots movements, we're struggling for a radical change in the capitalist system.

As for the two theologies, ours is still very timid and small before what's being produced in North America. I'd like to learn more about North American and African theology, but I also think we have something very specific to contribute.

*In an article on black women and Afro-American theology, you wrote about a "new way of doing theology." What is this "new way"?*

It's new because of the new subject doing this theology—women, black women. And those of us who have access to the university must develop this new method. Women have a very profound and incarnate experience of God. Our work is to listen to women and systematize this manifestation of God in women's lives and hearts, making it part of our theology.

This is new!

All of this has been very suffocated among our black people—our very bodies, our culture, the way we celebrate, the way we encounter God. Our body was always a slave body, a sacrificed body, a body given to work and exploitation. After slavery, our bodies were exploited by the capitalist system and seen as a place of profit-making through exploited labor. And when it was in the interest of the ruling powers, they called ours a "rebellious body."

Our body is also seen as a source of pleasure for anyone who wants to take advantage of it, yet hypocritically our body is also seen as the place of sin and perdition because it is "sensual" and "provocative." Because the black person's body was given to sensuality, it couldn't be a religious body, a consecrated body.

Today we're struggling to recognize the beauty of this body. Our body reveals the creative beauty of God. We have to seriously criticize the way the body has been abused and viewed. We don't look down on our sensuality. On the contrary, our body is the place we meet God! The place of revelation!

This valuing of the body can't just remain at the level of discourse, but has to be put into practice. If you look at our celebrations, we sing, we dance, we move. We celebrate with our whole body, recuperating the value of the body, recovering a unified vision of black women and men.

*Would you say that the church fears the human body, especially women's bodies?*

In the course of church history, we entered into dualism where our religion was of the soul, saving souls. Affectivity and sexuality were forgotten. Yet the church should be the very place of affect, caring, embraces, meeting, kissing! In recovering this, we're recovering the dignity of the human person.

Even in religious life, from my own experience, they negated this dimension of our corporeality. You consecrate your life to God—your will, your desires, your spirit in the hands of God. But, they didn't speak about consecrating your body.

What is a consecrated body? This is what we're searching for.

*What is it like to be a woman, especially a black woman, in Brazil today?*

The first problem is the awareness of being women. It seems that when a woman becomes a mother, a wife, she forgets all other dimensions of her life —she forgets that she's still a woman, a lover, a companion, a human being!

Also, there is so much domestic violence against women, where the husband thrashes the woman, sometimes beating her to death.

There's also the problem of education. In Brazil you often hear, especially regarding black women, "Women don't need to study." Super intelligent women don't have the opportunity to continue studying.

Then there's health. Women don't know their own bodies! When you don't understand your body very well, you don't love your body, and then others see this and take advantage of your body. This happens with women's bodies in relationships with their husbands, partners, even with their medical doctors. In Brazil many women are sterilized by their own doctors without even knowing it! The victims of this are usually from the poorest classes.

There's also the great difficulty of the participation of women. For example, while the great majority of CEB members are women, we don't participate in decision-making. Women work overtime—a double or triple day's work at home and then more work in the church community and the grassroots movements. Their partners don't understand this and force the woman to stop any activism outside the home.

Because of all this, it's difficult to organize ourselves as women. To poorer women, women's groups seem like a bourgeois thing, something the First World bothers with. Our women's group is reflecting on these very questions.

*Wealthy women also suffer abuse and discrimination. Have you seen women reaching across the class and race barriers to struggle for liberation together?*

I work with women in general and specifically with black women, and I sense a big difference. Among women, even though we don't like to admit it, relationships of domination can also exist—race and class.

For example, when a woman employer is with her maid, she's hardly going to be thinking, "Here is a woman, a companion, a friend in the struggle." No! The relationship there is employer and maid. And in Brazil, the great majority of domestic employees are black women. This reproduces a relationship of racial and class domination. Do you see?

So I think there will only be a meeting place if we respect each other's differences. In Brazil, it's usually the black women who stay at home, taking care of the house and children, so that white women can leave and be activists with feminist movements! So, even the feminist movements are made on the sacrifices of many other women—usually poor and black!

*Working with the CEBs, what do you think will happen to the communities if they continue to lose support from the institutional church?*

It's hard to talk about the future. I can only speak from what I feel in my heart: I believe in a God who reveals Godself in the life of the CEBs, a God for whom the CEBs are a privileged place of revelation for the world.

If we recover the word of God, we see that the Hebrew people many times saw everything completely closed off to them. This is how we feel today—if you look, you'll see a completely closed future. But I also believe that the God we profess is not a God of pomp, a flashy God of the multitudes. The God we profess is the God of the remnant, Israel, a small group of the little people, the poor, the People of God.

So, on one side, I see a fairly closed future. But, on the other side, I believe that the very situation we're living today—complete insecurity, fear of the future—is the privileged place of God's revelation! The communities began with euphoria and enthusiasm, but also with very strong roots—that is, the strong presence of the laity. They cannot be extinguished by decree. Nothing of the sort!

I believe this is *irreversible.* And we are taking tiny but decisive steps in this direction. I don't believe we will be turned around!

*You felt instinctually drawn to the poor at a very young age. What would you say to others who are trying to make concrete their concern for the poor?*

The option for the poor can be lived out differently by each person. I try to live this option radically, but this is a gift, a grace from God. Anyone can make this option!

Sometimes even those who have money manage to have a close identification with the poor. But you can't simply say "I'm going to do it." You have to really open your heart! That's why it's a grace, a gift, a call from God.

I see the option for the poor as a change in our social position. You choose to begin to think about things from the perspective of the poor. Often this becomes a change not just in social place, but in geographic place. That is, if you want to opt for the poor you must at least have contact with these poor persons. Sometimes, not always, you also have to live with these poor persons, share in their lives.

Sometimes I actually feel pain because I share in the very needs and wants of the poor. While we want to help the poor get out of the situation they are in, our very identification makes us participate in the "non-means" of the life of the poor.

For example, a neighbor was sick once, and I didn't have a car to take her to the hospital or the money for a taxi! You see, you begin to share a little bit in the misery of others. If I was still with the Franciscan sisters, I would only need to call the hospital and speak with a sister, and they would send an ambulance.

When we opt for the poor, we often lose much of our social prestige. This is very, very tough. My option for the poor has brought about many changes in my life.

*Have you gained something as well as having lost something?*

Yes! Friends! I've lost many, many friends, and have completely different friends today. The people are so affectionate, so mindful. I've had so many experiences of this. My neighbors have nothing to bring us, but they find a little tomato to give.

I think many wealthy people lack this sense of sharing, of fraternity. People who have everything think they are self-sufficient. But when you don't have everything, you need one another.

*Do you have a message for people in the First World?*

The relationship between North and South is marked by a great distance—geographical, racial and social distance. It is a relationship of exclusion. So the first thing we want is to be respected—respected as a Latin American people, as a Brazilian people, as women, as black people.

Beyond respect, I believe in a relationship of solidarity. I think solidarity comes through a change of place—leaving where you are a bit. You have to move from the place of imperialism to the place of brother and sister, friendship and equality.

It is also very important to really believe in each other. The other is not "underdeveloped" or "ignorant"! The other is simply other—different from myself. But the other also has part of the truth! This is true for all relationships—U.S./Brazil, men/women, blacks/whites. When we recognize each other's truth, we are able to meet one another in solidarity.

And this liberation comes at a high price—sometimes our very lives. But I call you to believe in this, to open yourselves to the future, to dream this dream—a dream that nourishes our lives and our struggle.

# 9

## Carlos Mesters

There is poverty in every human life. Inside of all our poverty, be it personal or social, we discover something of God.

The deepest poverty—the "nothing" within—brings us before God. That is, without God sustaining us, we are nothing.

*Carlos Mesters was born in Holland, where he became a Carmelite. He came to Brazil in 1949 to study, then was sent to Rome and Jerusalem to study Scripture, and returned to Brazil in 1963. After teaching in a Sao Paulo seminary for six years, he was transferred to Belo Horizone. Due to the repression of the 1970s, he stopped teaching at a formal level and began to work in parishes, giving Bible courses to the people. For the past twenty years he has worked at the Center for Bible Studies (CEBI) in Belo Horizonte, training pastoral leaders and assisting the region's CEBs.*

*Having read several small booklets by Carlos Mesters that present an interpretation of the Bible from the perspective of the poor, I had expected to meet a real firebrand; instead, I met a quiet and unassuming scholar-of-the-people. His most well-known work today is* Defenseless Flower: A New Reading of the Bible *(Orbis, 1989).*

*Frei Carlos and I met at a Carmelite retreat house in Jacarepaqua, outside of Rio, where he was attending a Carmelite conference. Before allowing me an interview, he insisted that I first rest, as I had been traveling all day.*

*During our interview we sat at a stone table in the garden below majestic trees. His voice was slow and gentle, taking every question, idea and challenge to heart, commenting from time to time on the plants, birds and flowers surrounding us. When I first*

*took out my tape recorder, he expressed caution and reluctance to*
*speak to a journalist. His words had been distorted before. By the*
*end of our conversation, just as I discovered he wasn't a firebrand,*
*he discovered that I wasn't an opportunistic journalist. As much a*
*theology student as a journalist, I explained.*

ঞ ঞ ঞ

Since the 1970s, the Latin American poor have been discovering the Bible.

They found in the Bible a mirror.

In the mirror, they discovered their own face, and began
reading the Bible from the perspective of their present day lives.
They discovered that the Bible doesn't say "Calm down, be toler-
ant—heaven comes later!" They discovered that the Bible says
the opposite: the God we believe in says, "I listen to the cry of
the poor."

The Bible is the gasoline hidden in the motor of the communities. If you take away the Bible, everything will die!

Those who would call the church of liberation too activist
have never been here. They don't know. The people pray so much!
If the car doesn't stop for gas it will stall in the middle of the road!

The people have a faith that feeds them through song and
prayer. The people have taught me this dimension of gratuity, of
contemplation, the prayerfulness of life.

Without this nourishment, we would become empty. Without prayer, I couldn't go on.

Today, in our difficult situation, we are seeing more clearly
that our motivations in the struggle have to be deepened. Merely
political or social motivations don't help us cross the desert. We
must look for more profound motivations in spirituality and mysticism. Only these will carry us through future difficulties.

ঞ ঞ ঞ

The poor read the Bible in the context of today.

The biblical scholar's vision is that the Bible has to be placed
in its original context, in the past. With science and analysis,

Two girls share a small Bible at a Sunday liturgy
organized by the CEBs in the community of
Christo Mestre (São Paulo).

scholarship helps us to not manipulate the Word of God or use it to prove anything we want.

But then we see that the situation of the past is really similar, though different, from today—problems of land, organization, community, the struggle against oppressive power and exploitation. The people discover companions in the Bible who are in the same struggle! Above all, they discover that God is on the side of those committed to the way of liberation, justice, fraternity.

I call the poor people's method of reading the Bible a "defenseless flower." That is, with scientific exegesis you can show that everything the poor do has little value. What the people say is immensely fragile.

But there is a power in weakness.

It's like the grass around you—one blade isn't worth anything! The poor's interpretation is like a blade of grass! Pull up one, and nothing changes. But many blades of grass together make the whole yard green! The people are like the wind. Your hand moves freely through air, yet the power of the wind can tear down trees!

This is the same for women who are beginning to interpret scripture. At first this new angle that women bring seems strange to people, and men trained in traditional exegesis will easily tear down a woman's exegesis.

The interpretation of the poor is fragile. Like the tree's underground roots. You can push this big tree here and it will never fall. Yet the tips of the roots are as tiny as your baby fingernail! And the more fragile the ends of the roots, the stronger the tree! The power of weakness again.

Though the interpretation of the poor is weak, it threatens many people.

Reading the Bible helps the people see that many things in the church and the world are not as God wants them to be. So they begin to organize themselves and disturb the pastor, the bishop, the government.

Even the institutional church seems afraid of this flower! But I don't think others need to be afraid! God reveals God's strength in weakness.

ⱴ ⱴ ⱴ

I have a lot of faith in the people.

It comes from this: the force of life is so strong. A young man and woman have a child—this is the force of life! I have great faith in the force of life!

Yet this life reveals itself in fragile ways.

The way to believe in God is to believe in life, in persons. We don't have anything else. You'll never run into God on the street corner! You'll meet persons! And here in Latin America, you'll meet poor persons.

ॐ ॐ ॐ

There's a poverty in every human life.

When we're aware of our limits, we're more open to change and conversion.

If our limits are at the individual level, like alcoholism or alienation, our awareness can provoke a change so that we can grow beyond this.

Here in Brazil, our limits are very much at the social level—hunger, homelessness. We struggle to become aware and change these things. But sometimes after engaging in a long social struggle, we realize that nothing grew inside of us. Maybe in the U. S. your limits are more at the personal level. But sometimes when you are struggling individually, you realize that you have to address the social dimension to arrive at the personal dimension.

Without integration of the personal and the social, we won't be full persons.

We may start at different points, but we arrive together.

The struggle is one.

ॐ ॐ ॐ

And the deepest poverty—the "nothing" within—brings us before God.

At the root of this poverty, we discover that without God sustaining us, we are nothing. And we all share this "nothing." No one can escape it.

This is where we are invited to struggle together. We're on the same team! There's a common cause at stake!

It doesn't help for us to fight against each other. Moreover, the moment I absolutize my view of things, I can't be enriched by anything. I'm sterile. Dialogue is so important, learning to listen to others, because every single person always has something to teach us. The poor person has so much to teach us!

The struggle, then, is against everything that dehumanizes life.

If I hit you, I am dehumanizing you, but much more than that, I'm dehumanizing myself. The moment I mistreat someone, I'm hurting myself more.

The struggle comes from the Bible—Jesus talked about it.

We have to struggle from the moment we wake up until we go to bed! When I'm weary and don't want to see anyone, and someone I don't like comes along, I have to struggle to welcome that person! When I see an injustice and am afraid and want to run away, I have to struggle to speak my word.

የ፦ የ፦ የ፦

My hope for the future is like the prophet Jeremiah.

Every person with their own little piece of land, where everyone can plant, live, have their parties, with life that overflows. This is the happiness of a people at peace, living from their work, in equality.

Maybe this will only happen with the resurrection! Maybe this is a utopia of the past. The world is much more complex today. Maybe some day . . .

Meanwhile, I'm sustained by my friends. By my commitments with people. By faith in God and reading the Word of God.

At times I don't hear, I don't see. But in my core, I know I must stay with this commitment. Abandoning it would be contrary to life.

I can't say I'm better than others. But at least I try to be faithful.

And I give thanks to God who carries me and receives my life.

የ፦ የ፦ የ፦

*Liberation theology has focused on the liberation of the poor. Do you believe women's liberation will become more important in this theology?*

*The poor community's reading of the Bible:* In a CEB Sunday liturgy in São Paulo, two young people share the youth group's reflection on the Bible readings, comparing the "News of the Bible" (L) to the "News of the People" (R). The Bible tells that "God created the world. God saw all of this was good. God shared this beautiful world with man and woman, etc." In the News of the People, however, "The price of bread went up. The price of the bus went up. In this country millions of children die of hunger. Brazil has a lot of land, but in the hands of a few people, etc."

I think that the root of all oppression is men over women. At their core, totalitarian systems are undergirded by the oppression of men over women. Families also and interpersonal relationships, where men dominate women. At times even women internalize this and let themselves be exploited. There will never be full and integral [holistic] liberation without permeating this at its depths.

*It also seems that even when people use inclusive language for men and women, they have difficulty accepting inclusive language for God.*

Language takes a long time to evolve. It takes a long time to change a name! In the Bible, when the people were in their worst situation, exile, God was called Mother, Father, Husband by the people. The people were the "bride of God"! All of these images appear!

But people change slowly, and our image of God may be the most difficult thing to change, because this is where we anchor our lives. This is the deepest part of our roots.

*Yet isn't society shaped and justified by our implicit or explicit image of God?*

Yes, I think all the politicians in Brazil use God. They always present themselves as the defenders of God. This is because power searches for its legitimation starting from God, religious legitimation.

This is where we need to show that God isn't with them, but with the poor. God reveals Godself in weakness. Jesus didn't criticize images of God as much as he showed an alternative image of God, which so inconvenienced people that they only let him speak for three years, then they eliminated him. Jesus revealed a face of God that bothered society profoundly!

I think the communities are walking with a new experience of God—a more human, more liberating face of God which disturbs some people. It also disturbs the church!

*How would you describe your own image of God?*

It's very difficult, difficult—I don't think I know how!

If you didn't have a mirror, would you know how to describe your face? No. Well, you might, but not with words. You'd only know how to describe your face from what other people say about it. But you can touch it!

We can touch God in experiences.

*When we look on at all of the recent conflicts between the Vatican and elements of the Latin American church, some people say it's because liberation theology is Marxist and others say that Rome is allied with the ruling elites. You intimate that Rome fears the new style of church emerging from the CEBs.*

Actually, I think each one of these explanations holds a little bit of the truth! When you take photographs from various angles, each one has a piece of truth. But I think at the core of the conflict is a question of power. Also the question of the option for the poor.

I believe that many of the arguments that come from Rome are invented. The very person who accuses the liberation theologians of Marxism also uses Marxism! Everyone uses it today. The Pope himself used it in his encyclical *On Human Work*, yet no one criticizes the Pope as being Marxist. But when you want to hit a dog, you always find a stick.

Behind it all is a fear of change. They're afraid that the people, the laity, will have a more significant role in the church, and that the places they gain won't have anymore meaning.

*With all this going on, do you have hope or fear for the future?*

In the long run, I have hope. No one can overthrow life.

But, in the short run, it's going to be difficult. The conservative bishops that are being appointed are using their heads—they're organizing and getting key positions. They have the many advantages, and 2000 years experience! We are like immigrants that arrive in another land where we don't have as much experience.

All of this calls us to deepen our reflection and action. It's like an off-season for fruit. The tree isn't dead, but we have to wait for another season to gather fruit. And not just the Christian communities are passing through very difficult times—the masses of Brazilian people also! Things in our country have almost come to a halt!

It's not a time to be discouraged—no! But, it is not an easy time either.


*Where does your hope come from?*

Look at history! In the time of Pius X, at the beginning of this century, there was a tremendous persecution against everything new. The people could hardly breathe anymore! But he died, and with time things changed again.

We've already lived through these moments many times before. Not only because leaders change, but because people can't endure living in a closed room for very long. Finally, even the one who ordered the window shut will say, "Open the window, we can't take it anymore!" This will happen again.

But we can't sit around waiting for it. We have to prepare for this moment to arrive.


*What are the most serious consequences of the nominations of conservative bishops and the disciplining of theologians?*

Little by little, the church is becoming more conservative, returning to a Christianity where the cleric controls things, where the people are stifled, and many officials lose some of their humanity. This is so unpleasant for us, especially for the communities of the poor where the church was being reborn, remade.

Today the most important support isn't going to the CEBs, but to the conservative international movements organized by Rome, like Opus Dei, the Charismatic movement, Communion and Liberation. I think this is a shame.


*Do you think a day will arrive when theologians don't accept silencing or that an actual schism will occur?*

I don't know. I think that in this century the schism isn't from the CEBs but from the right—Lefebvre and others.

No, the communities won't split off. They'll continue struggling. In Nicaragua, for example, a bishop asked the people, "Why are you leaving the church?" They said, "By no means! We *are* the church!"

Everyone doesn't necessarily agree with everyone else, but there has to be space for dialogue. Just the fact of being a bishop doesn't mean one has the right to impose thought on others. A bishop also has to dialogue.

*Both Catholic and historical Protestant churches in Brazil express concern about the rapid growth of Pentecostal churches, which focus on the Bible and healing. How do you explain their appeal?*

While some of these churches have a fundamentalist reading of the Bible, which is harmful, they also have a good dimension. That is, one million Brazilians leave the Catholic church every year for other churches because they find new strength from the Bible and gain the courage to break away from the priest.

As a human decision, this can be a really good thing! However, many of these people fall into places that brainwash and dehumanize them, which is a shame.

Also, when people come from the countryside to the city, they're completely lost and feel abandoned. The Pentecostal churches welcome them, call them sister and brother—they recover a name, a history. We talk about an option for the poor, but it's the poorest of the poor who are going to these other churches.

Fortunately, a few of these Pentecostal and charismatic churches are opening to a more liberationist perspective. However, there's still a long way to go. Too often these churches are conservative, rightist, contrary to the interests of the people.

*What have you gained from your own work with poor communities?*

The poor have a great humanity. There's such a happiness that you don't know where it came from! There's a sense of justice, of sharing, of faith. This is all in the midst of poor people whose lives are terribly dehumanized!

For example, one time a poor person said to me, "When I moved to the city, I have the greatest sorrow when I pass a poor person begging, and I don't have anything to give him! I go and hide in my house so he won't see my face. The worst thing in the world is to have nothing to share with a person poorer than myself."

*What does the option for the poor mean to you?*

The option for the poor doesn't mean that everyone has to be poor. No! Nor does it mean looking down on the rich.

The option for the poor means that we struggle so that all the goods God gave the world are distributed so that all people can have life. We should all agree on this not because we're Christian, but simply because we're human! It's a human right for people, the poor, to be respected.

For a long time the church only spoke from the side of the rich—about giving alms to the poor. Today, in speaking from the side of the poor, they speak to all of us.

Before, the rich said to the poor, "Why are you poor?" And many Brazilians said "Indians and blacks are poor because they're lazy!" Today the poor say to the rich, "Why are you rich?" In Brazil we have poor people who rise at 4 A.M. and return to bed at midnight, working the entire day. Yet when this man retires at seventy-five, he doesn't have enough resources to support his wife!

The poor work harder than many other people, but the whole organization of society doesn't favor them. If my father says, "I struggled to earn what's mine. I'm rich because I deserve it." Well it's also because the laws favored him! A friend's father could say, "I struggled and didn't earn anything"—and he may be more intelligent and industrious than my father!

The poor, just by the fact that they are poor, without saying anything to us, tell us, "The way the world is organized is wrong, because there's no place for us. We are equal to you." When I see that a tiny part of humanity lives well, and ninety percent don't live well, something is wrong in God's world.

The option for the poor is the option for equality, fraternity, justice.

One time, I visited a poor woman dying of cancer in a tiny home in Belo Horizonte. When I left her house I saw huge trucks carrying expensive minerals back and forth. I saw that this world of commerce and profit reflected a certain vision of life. I thought, if this vision of life doesn't have room for the poor woman dying of cancer, something is terribly wrong. She has the right to participate in this society.

*Does this mean that privileged people have to renounce their privilege?*

People must have in their minds and hearts, in their hands and feet this cause of life. If I studied to be a lawyer, I should place my studies at the service of this project. That doesn't mean that I have to abandon everything I own. If I give everything to the poor and there are 100 poor persons, tomorrow there will be 101—nothing changes!

I have to use my mind and reason and everything God gave me in such a way that, little by little, we can provoke a change.

*How do you think wealthy people will come to this awareness, especially if they are born into the world-view you described, seeing the poor as lazy?*

I really don't know. Jesus found difficulty here. He said it was easier for a camel to pass through the eye of a needle than for a rich person to enter the Kingdom of God. Then he told the parable of Lazarus and the rich man. It seems Jesus didn't see much possibility for the conversion of the wealthy.

Who knows? Maybe the Kingdom is the CEBs, and it's difficult for a rich person to enter the communities, where the poor are the ones who share so naturally.

Maybe conversion will come through a crisis—ecological, demographical, atomic danger. Thirty years from now North America and Europe will be five percent of the world population, and they won't be able to maintain this paradise of theirs. The poor populations will explode and the water will overflow!

*Do you think the poor have something to teach the rich in this regard?*

Yes! I came from Holland, thinking I'd bring the Good News as a missionary. These forty years I've learned that the mission is also from here to Holland! You see, the poor have something that First World people have lost. I don't know what. But many people who come here feel something that's lost there. Something to do with life.

The wind has changed: now there's a mission from the poor to the rich!

Missions were always articulated from the North to the South. The mission from South to North is just beginning. It's like a ship that's facing North-South, but the wind has changed. It's difficult to move the ship because the canal is narrow. And it has to become a two-way street. But the wind has changed!

*What message would you like to share with people in the First World?*

I don't have the courage to say what I'm thinking! Who am I to give advice?

At least I would say this: don't be afraid of freedom. The people in the United States were born from freedom, yet it seems they fear other people's freedom. They keep us inside a system that allows them to have freedom, but we don't have freedom! You have a constitution and respect institutions. Please, don't fear our freedom.

I say this especially to the people. At times we don't distinguish enough between the government, or, better to say the system, and the people. The people we meet are completely different from the system.

*What specifically can we do to be in more solidarity with you?*

So many ways! Poverty is a global problem, with causes both here and there. This invites more than our solidarity with the poor. This makes it seem as if people who weren't poor had everything good and now have to help the poor.

We need a two-sided solidarity. Solidarity as a commitment to the fundamental values of human life, that help us struggle here and there. The struggle is one—we're not enemies in this!

# 10

# TEREZA MARIA CAVALCANTI

Liberation must be holistic. Not just economic liberation, but liberation from sin—which encompasses everything. Liberation from our prisons, our selfishness, our insecurities and prejudices.

I wouldn't say liberation from our conflicts because liberation itself brings conflict! To the extent that we work through the conflict, it helps the process of liberation.

*Tereza Maria Cavalcanti was born in Rio de Janeiro in 1943. At the time I interviewed Tereza, she was finishing her doctorate in theology at the Catholic Pontifical University (PUC) in Rio. She graduated one year later with honors.*

*The mother of three children, Tereza is a professor and coordinator of the Graduate Department of Theology at the PUC. She is also the coordinator of the Spirituality Program at CEBI—the Center for Biblical Studies where Carlos Mesters works. Tereza has long worked in Bible ministry among the CEBs and also serves as a resource person for women's groups. In addition to writing texts on the popular reading of the Bible, she has also published articles on the spirituality of family.*

*Like many others interviewed here, Tereza was a student at the time of the military takeover in 1964. While studying philosophy in São Paulo, she joined the Catholic University Youth movement, which resisted the dictatorship.*

*While I was in Rio de Janeiro conducting interviews, Tereza and her family graciously offered me hospitality. The family lived*

Tereza and her husband, Teófilo, outside of their home in Rio de Janeiro.

*in a comfortable, middle-class neighborhood of Rio. In the midst of these comfortable surroundings, Tereza lives without pretense, ever aware of the responsibilities she must balance—family, teaching and working with poor communities and women's groups.*

૪૨ ૪૨ ૪૨

I was raised in a family very open to social questions, and their social vision really formed me.

My grandfather was always politically active with the left. And my mother, along with raising twelve children, always had projects going to help the poor, empowering them to be independent. My father, who taught aeronautics, was fired from his university job because he wouldn't denounce students who were later imprisoned by the military.

Because of my family background, my faith has always been linked with social ethics. I've always had a strong sense of ethical indignation before social injustice.

૪૨ ૪૨ ૪૨

My doctoral work is on the grassroots method of reading the Bible developed by Carlos Mesters.

When you read a book by Carlos Mesters, instead of finding the theological categories difficult, we theologians have difficulty understanding the popular categories he uses. He writes about the seed, the flower, the cow—images!

He reverses directions. He brings the people *inside* of theology instead of bringing theology to the people.

As a teacher, I've also been very influenced by the Paulo Freire literacy method.

Teaching literacy through Freire's method brought me in direct contact with the people, their thought, their self-expression. My students had such great enthusiasm for being able to participate in what was called "conscientization"—people discovering through reading, writing and dialogue what was going on in society.

૪૨ ૪૨ ૪૨

A common view of Rio de Janeiro shows both the downtown high-rises and, in the foreground, the hillside *favelas*.

Recently I've become more involved in women's issues.

I find the word feminist ambiguous.

The connotation it's taken on in society is opposition to *machista*. The word feminine isn't acceptable either because it carries the traditional connotation of sweetness and submission.

We need a word to say that we are starting with women and not men. No word is adequate! We say "from a woman's perspective."

Maybe anti-sexist is the word.

Even within liberation theology, we cannot speak of a revolution in awareness of gender, but a waking-up. For so long liberation theology gave priority to social class. Now it's starting to open to other problems—culture, sexuality, etc.

New women theologians are starting to fill this gap. But if you look at a collection of liberation theology books, you'll see eighty books by men and three by women. Our numbers are few, and when there are meetings, women speak less.

If a women does get up to say something, the men begin to laugh. Or they look to see if she's pretty or ugly. Or if a woman's more combative, they say, "It's because she's frustrated in her marriage!" or "She needs a man!"

Sure, if there's a handsome man who gets up to speak, the women react—they enjoy seeing a beautiful man! But I think it's inappropriate when men demand that a woman be beautiful or feminine, in their opinion of "feminine," in order to speak in public.

Even the liberation theologians have a hard time arguing with women on an equal level.

ও ও ও

It has been so enriching for me to work with women!

In the beginning, it was like creating a new eye, a new ear. Beginning to look at things from the perspective of women and women's specific problems, which are always related with life—survival, health, children.

Yes, children, for example.

To speak of children is to speak of being inconvenienced.

You can plan your day, but if you have a child, this child will mix up your whole day. He can become sick or wet her pants—at times you least expect it! You have to always be attentive to the most trivial daily necessities.

This opens a person to greater *availableness.*†

It's difficult to balance everything—my family, my home, my profession and my ministry. I seek equilibrium in all this. My husband helps and truly respects my work. And I thank God that our financial situation allows me to be outside of the house—we have a maid. But I still have to turn down many opportunities because of family life.

ॐ ॐ ॐ

I think the option for the poor, which is essential to liberation theology, was made real by many people in my generation before there was even a word for it.

People let themselves be caught up in social problems through a concrete encounter with the poor. From there, they changed their whole life vision, their politics, even their habits. Many became politically committed and were persecuted or even killed, imprisoned, exiled.

Some went to live among the poor, especially nuns, priests and some lay persons. Others concluded that it wasn't worth it to leave the middle-class and become a worker if you were displacing a poorer worker.

In my view, the option for the poor means opting for the *causes* of the poor. Not that I become materially poor like the poor are, but that I put all my resources at the cause of the poor and assist the struggle of the poor.

And the struggle for liberation has many faces.

You see, the political struggle, the struggle within the church, my personal struggle are all part of the option for the poor. My personal struggle is to listen to the poor, to value what they say, and to learn from them. I always learn so much!

ॐ ॐ ॐ

Liberation must be integral (holistic). Not just economic liberation, but liberation from sin—liberation from poverty, from insecurity, from selfishness.

For example, I belong to a group of therapists who work with body and music therapy. This is also a project of liberation! Just like economic liberation and women's liberation, the personal and spiritual realm is important.

Our interior lives are very important.

---

†Tereza's actual word was *disponibilidade*, a disposition of openness in which one is accessible, available and willing to be inconvenienced by the needs or requests of another person or event.

I wouldn't say liberation from our conflicts because liberation itself brings conflict! To the extent that we work through the conflict, it helps the process of liberation.

At times I think the poor are more disposed to develop an interior life because they don't get everything on a silver platter. They have to struggle. They need an inner resolve and strength.

Rich people are more passive before reality. Whatever difficulty they encounter, they buy their way out. But you can't buy happiness!

In this sense, we who are not poor need liberation from our panaceas and the illusions that deceive us—believing that joy is in consuming, that to be fulfilled in my profession I must step on others. I will lie, cheat and rob, but in a technically planned out way that goes perfectly undetected! But, in doing this, I'm hurting myself and my children.

Interior liberation is very important—freeing ourselves of the false securities that technological development brings.

In this sense, perhaps women are also closer to the interior life because, part of the time, we inevitably have to attend to our bodies.

And our body is a limit.

It's both a limit and the means of liberation, because my body gives me access to the greatest marvels of the world!

In our highly technical civilization, I tend to lose the sense of my limitations. I think the computer will solve everything, or speed will solve things.

🙒 🙒 🙒

I have such a deep desire for spirituality!

I believe the key experience of spirituality is just that—our desire for spirituality. We're living in an important moment of global spirituality. I pray with all people! With Spiritists, Buddhists, people doing Tai Chi. Even people without religion have this desire.

You see, my husband isn't Christian. But he has these moments of an interior life. He participates with me on retreats. And we have a profound level of sharing.

I think it's even good that he's not Christian!

I am much more "coherent" in my Christianity because he challenges and questions me without condemning me. We have a stimulating dialogue—questioning each other without judging each other.

There was a time in my life where it was difficult to pray.

Even now, there are moments when God is very vague.

But at the core it's still God.

ᛞᛞ ᛞᛞ ᛞᛞ

*Where would you critique liberation theology?*

I think liberation theology needs to deepen its contemplative side, not in the sense of a removed "spiritualist" contemplation, but a contemplation that comes from the experience of suffering and from the failure of our efforts.

A while ago, Nicaragua was a model of success for us. All of a sudden, it comes to a failure of sorts—economically, socially, politically. Some very important values can emerge from within this experience of suffering, of not conquering power. A reflection about power seen from those who don't have power, the other side of power.

*In your opinion, what are the consequences of the recent actions from the Vatican for the church of liberation in Brazil?*

The first consequence is the loss of power and the feelings of insecurity and abandonment, of not being understood. This shakes up our faith. Because if we preach a God who hears the cry of the poor, God the liberator, the moment arrives when we realize that we aren't seeing this happen in our history.

But perhaps we're living at a time when something truly profound will emerge—maybe something that will reach a universal level. Maybe in these moments there is a faith that assumes the cross, that assumes loss, even abandonment. Like we see in the Suffering Servant in Isaiah, or in the abandonment of Jesus on the cross.

*What do you think is at the center of the conflict with the Vatican?*

I think there are two concepts of church. One is a pyramid, the church as a highly structured society with a well-defined

O E MORRA DE DESGOSTO.
PELA
VIDA
Viva
8 de MARÇO
DIA
INTERNACIONAL
DA MULHER
PELA
PAZ.

hierarchy. The other style is circular, with the people as a community. Here, the question of fidelity to the Gospel has primacy over that of power. Power is in relation to service, service being more important.

Now, the more communitarian model can pose problems for unity. Where power and authority are well-defined, unity is guaranteed. When there's freedom, such the Protestant Reformation, you run the risk of less cohesion of the church body.

That's how I understand it—the conflict over an emphasis on power or service.

*Some people say that the CEBs are falling apart. Do you have hope for the future of the CEBs?*

Reflecting as a woman, I've rediscovered the parable of the virgins and the lamps. My impression is that the people at the base have a profound energy—an oil that lights their lamp—because they've encountered centuries and centuries of suffering. I think the discouragement before the loss of our few victories is more typical of the middle class and intellectuals who are thinking, "Let's get into power."

The poor were never on the side of power. So they've developed mechanisms to confront the opposite side of power, the disillusionment of their hopes and expectations. They have great reserves of strength.

On the other hand, there are many articles by theologians saying, "The CEBs have lost their strength! They're weak and discouraged!" They make serious criticisms of the CEBs, saying that they haven't maintained a language in accord with the people like the Pentecostal sects have. They're blaming the CEBs.

The CEBs have made mistakes, but now is precisely the moment to value the completely new thing that's emerged in the CEBs—people organizing themselves, the democracy within the communities and in all of the organizations where people from the CEBs are present. The CEBs inaugurated this respect for power sharing! This is something absolutely new and should be appreciated and continued.

Graffiti in the town of Rio Branco celebrates International Women's Day in the Americas: "For Life, For Peace—Long Live the 8th of March, International Woman's Day!"

We're in a period of suffering, but we have to carry it forward.

*Are theologians beginning to work with the ecological movement? Do you believe women have something particular to contribute to this struggle?*

Yes, but what's more important than the theology is the practice—the concrete struggle to defend the land, to defend small farmers, to defend the Indians. The Indians are the ones who preserve our rainforests!

Because of their very poverty, many women in rural areas have developed alternative nutrition and herbal medicine. The *benzedeira* [faith healer] is also an important figure in people's lives. These women have the gift of healing the body through simple methods they learned from their grandmothers. These are the people who know how to live from the land without destroying it. The people also gain gradual independence from formal health care institutions this way.

*You described a certain unwillingness on the part of male theologians to seriously accept women into theology. What do you think causes this?*

I think the men feel a lot of ambiguity. Even when they want to value women, they feel some fear. They want women to have their word, but they feel insecure when women speak with competence. They have a hard time acknowledging the truth of a woman's idea, especially if it's different from what the men already stated.

They generally assume that women haven't arrived at their level of competence. And often this is true! Women are only now arriving at the intellectual realm and studying theology. But this doesn't mean that women aren't right when they discover new things.

*I was surprised to see that even the Brazilian Bishops' 1990 Campaign on Women refers to God as Father throughout all of its texts.*

I think that this question of language is less important here than in the U.S. Here the priority is life. And to defend life, which is always threatened, you have to organize. So more important than using language of "men and women" are the actual bonds of solidarity between people who suffer, who begin to discover a new model of society and church. In this solidarity, it's women who take the initiative.

This linking of women and life, of women and solidarity is something new that we can bring to you in the U.S.! Language is important, but it comes later.

*Do you think First and Third World women theologians have mutual contributions to make to each other?*

I think our theology has been so marked by Marxist categories, where social analysis is so important, that it's important for us also consider gender issues. Analyzing society only according to rich and poor isn't enough.

First World theologians have given us important tools—a more scientific vision and the hermeneutics of suspicion before patriarchal and *machista* texts. Elizabeth Schüssler-Fiorenza is excellent, and she's open to the social question as well. That is, the early community of Jesus wasn't just open to men and women, but to prostitutes, the poor, beggars, street people. All marginalized people.

*What contributions are Latin American women making to feminism in the U.S.?*

It's difficult here to distinguish the contribution of women from that of Third World women and men.

An important discovery is gratuity. That is, giving time and space for what's not anticipated, what comes from God, from the future. Availability (*disponibilidade*)—not being a prisoner to our projects and plans. And hospitality. This is an important quality and character of our people. Their houses are always open!

There's also unity and solidarity. For example, we know about the feminization of poverty in the U.S. I've heard that there's a lot of child abuse because women aren't prepared to take care of children and society is not affirming of children's reality. So, women feel alone and despair and abuse children. Here, when someone suffers, the climate facilitates open houses. Women will call out and seek help from their neighbors. There seems to be more solidarity among women here.

Enter the men. *Machismo* here is terrible! There's an enormous level of violence from boyfriends and fathers—and especially from the husbands. This often happens when the woman becomes more independent. She goes to church meetings and returns strengthened, and he doesn't accept it.

But sometimes, after the initial violence, the men notice that the home and family is improving because of her community involvement. He sees that even he gains when the woman has more freedom. At times they even join the struggle together. But, many other stories don't end this way. Some women die.

There's so much suffering, so much violence against women!

*In class terms, do you think the poor and the rich have something to offer each other in the liberation process?*

When you say rich in a society with the level of misery here, we must ask what rich means. If it means to have a house, a telephone, an automobile, food, the opportunity to study—the minimum infrastructure to live comfortably, no problem. But we don't call that rich here. We call that "people of means"—like all people should live. These people can share their material and cultural goods in common.

But the super-rich before the poor are like the Gospel story about Lazarus and the rich man—there is only condemnation and a warning for the rich to be converted. That is, the super-rich have to stop being rich because it's a scandal! There are no super-rich people who don't dominate other people.

In fact, I think rich people always have much more to receive from the poor than the poor from the rich. I've learned so much through my work with the people. There's a certain happiness that's constant among them. They love celebrations and they don't economize for parties! This doesn't seem reasonable, but it's an experience of gratuity, of *disponibilidade*, of not clinging to goods, of sharing. The black people are also close to this sense of celebration and happiness, this capacity to always laugh.

This is why I say our feminism is a feminism that traded rancor for humor, because women who are suffering and discovering their emancipation know how to laugh before the facts! Laugh before men! It is a stance of joy before life.

*Do you see many possibilities for people from other countries to be in solidarity with the people of Brazil?*

There are many Americans already doing many things!

I saw them go to Nicaragua, putting themselves on the border and risking their lives. This shows there are people in the U.S. who think very differently from the majority, positioning themselves critically, risking their lives to be consistent.

It's really important for us to know that there are people in wealthier countries who are in solidarity with the more dominated and suffering countries. This strengthens our own struggle here!

*What message would you like to bring to people in the First World?*

I only want to say this: ours is a common struggle. A struggle for life, for human dignity, for spirituality. The struggle to preserve the species, to preserve the land, to preserve the planet.

We share the same struggle.

# 11

## CLODOVIS BOFF

One time we were raising awareness about the elections when the police surrounded us with machine guns and threw us in jail. We stayed the night, until the bishop intervened and they freed us.

But, for that night in jail, no one was afraid. We prayed! We sang church songs! We gave cheers! Because when you have this conviction, this faith, this option, you have no more fear of death.


*Clodovis Boff is a Servite priest and theologian living in Rio de Janeiro. In 1964, he and other young seminarians prayed their rosaries in the streets to thank the military government for saving them from communism and anarchy. After studying in Europe, where he met exiled students, workers and political prisoners, Clodovis returned to Brazil in passionate opposition to the military regime.*

*For twelve years Clodovis alternated between six months of intellectual work, writing and teaching, and six months of work at the base, accompanying CEBs and organizing unions in the Amazon among the Indigenous, farmers and rubber-tappers. Today Clodovis spends his months of pastoral work with urban workers in the periphery of São Paulo, rather than in the Amazon.*

*Though his prolific theological writings have not been censored by the Vatican like those of his brother, Leonardo, Cardinal Eugenio Sales of Rio has barred Clodovis from teaching at the Pontifical University of Rio (PUC). Clodovis still directs doctoral students at the PUC. He is also a professor at the Franciscan Theology Institute (ITF) in Petropolis, north of Rio, and teaches a course in "Social Mariology" every two years in Rome.*

*During our interview in the front parlor of his monastery, Clodovis' presence fills the room as he speaks in exclamation points! Hands flying, roaming, fishing for words, he laughs, shouts, whispers, waits, then laughs again. Clodovis is like a river with wild waterfalls and deep silent places. Later, he takes me to his study, laughing heartily as he shows me a photo of himself with the Pope next to photos of himself and his brother Leonardo with Fidel Castro.*

*There is something in Clodovis' personality and presence that reminds me of Pedro Casaldáliga. Both have faced prison and death threats. Both share a remarkable freedom—a rare fearlessness before death that allows them to exuberantly savor life.*

ৡ ৡ ৡ

I come from a very big family of Italian descent. Leonardo was the oldest boy, the third oldest in all, while I was the eighth of eleven children.

We grew up in a farming village in the southern Brazilian state of Santa Catarina. As children, we worked in the fields with my mother. My mother was completely illiterate. She awoke in us a life of faith and a love for work.

My father was a primary school teacher. He was very cultured and loved books. He made us read and awoke in all of us an intellectual vocation. From a religious perspective, my father was—well, he wasn't a practicing believer. He was a free thinker and very critical in relation to the institutional church—priests, bishops, cardinals and Rome. At the same time, he had a great love for justice. A great love for the poor and marginalized.

I remember a situation when I was a child.

A black family, leasing land from the church, was pressured by the pastor to leave the church land. My father thought this was an abuse, a lack of humanity. He opposed this and really stirred up tension with the pastor and the church.

He had quite a spirit—independent, critical.

This seems prophetic, doesn't it?

Of course, this all shaped Leonardo and the rest of us.

On a shelf in his study, below family portraits and
religious icons, Clodovis displays a photograph of
himself meeting the Pope next to images of himself and Leonardo visiting with Fidel Castro.

ৡ ৡ ৡ

I entered the seminary when I was twelve—the Servants of Mary, a small mendicant order from the time of St. Francis.

The formation in the archdiocesan seminary of Rio was academic and aristocratic—alienated from the reality of the people. It was preparing us for a "happy" Brazil of the privileged minorities.

Only when I went to study in Belgium and met exiled Brazilian students who suffered political persecution did I discover the Brazil of the poor, the eighty percent, the Brazil of conflict, of the oppressed. The real Brazil, not the rose-tinted Brazil that the seminary put in our heads. We began holding clandestine courses at night, analyzing the national predicament and organizing our opposition to this situation.

When the superior suggested I do my doctorate in theology, I chose to return to Brazil to immerse myself in concrete reality.

So I spent a year in the Amazon state of Acre, in 1969, when the CEBs were beginning. Then I spent two years in the periphery of São Paulo, working with students who held clandestine meetings with workers and the grassroots movements. These years, 1970 to 1973, were the harshest period of the dictatorship—the police even tapped the monastery phone!

We began to work with political prisoners, a very delicate, dangerous work, because we'd bring messages to and from the political prisoners.

This was an important period in my life because I made a complete rupture with an alienating formation and firmly chose a committed formation. I went from an abstract, universalist theology to an incarnated, committed theology.

When I finally returned to Europe to complete my doctorate in theology, I brought a completely different perspective—a spirit of war, of rage. I had little intellectual discipline. I wanted to transform reality overnight—in a volcanic manner!

I hadn't yet discovered the historical process—the patience of consciousness-raising and organizing the poor. I discovered that in my pastoral work in the Amazon.

ৡ ৡ ৡ

Without a doubt, the most important stage in my conversion was discovery of the poor person as a victim—not the by-product of nature, destiny or the will of God. But the *victim* of structural injustices—oppressed, impoverished.

This meant a fundamental rupture in my whole life!

I began to reflect on the Bible, church tradition and dogmas starting from this optic of the poor. All of my thought became fermented by this massive, dark, heavy oppression of the poor.

Really, the birthplace of liberation theology is the meeting of faith with poverty and oppression. It is when you, as a person of faith, meet the poor of the *favelas* and ask, "What's the meaning of God here? What does it mean to be church?" From this collision of your faith and concrete reality, liberation theology is born!

At the core, this is a very prophetic theology, carrying on the thinking of the prophets: "You are oppressing the widow and orphan! Your hands are stained with blood!"

Once awake, you are sensitized intellectually and spiritually—your prayer, even religious life is marked by the cry of the poor, the hope for a new society.

Now, this experience of the poor is nourished by and becomes rooted in real communities of poor persons. We're bound with two knots—our alliance with the poor and our work at the base.

After ten years of absorbing this, you no longer need ideological reasons to explain that the cause is just. The reality of oppression begans to be part of your blood and skin. A reason beyond all reasons!

This is why, when you delve into this alliance, this option, you go unto death. Unto death. Until martyrdom.

ະ⁄ ະ⁄ ະ⁄

In truth, for me personally, this whole process took place within my vocation as a religious, even as a priest. I've desired to follow Jesus. When I discovered the crushed and the hungry, I discovered that the dream and will of God wasn't realized!

When you see rubber-tappers expelled from their land, cheated by the rich land owners, then arriving in the city destitute, buying land and being expelled yet again, and crushed by the police—this horrid level of violence! And here you are—raised with sensitivity to the "Gospel," "human charity" and "respect for the other." Then you see that reality is contrary to all of these values!

This creates a collision—it stirs indignation! Rebellion!

The spirit of a revolutionary is born from this contrast between our ideals and the reality around us that doesn't match
them. This awareness of reality gives faith a courage to confront
criticism, persecution, death threats, prison.

Even within the community, the order or the church, people
don't understand you. They think you're crazy, sick, radical—
even subversive! But you don't let yourself be bothered by this
because the very cause takes hold of you.

It sustains you.

This reality also gives faith a very incarnational, concrete
meaning. You say, what do these poor people want? For them,
the Reign of God means a piece of land, a piece of bread, even a
simple literacy program.

But, the people also dream of a new world, a kind society,
universal love. They hope and believe that the rich will convert
and will help them.

భ భ భ

The ultimate root of my spirituality isn't a poor person. It's
not political, nor a new society, nor anything exterior. It's a fire
there inside! It's an experience—a pulse of life, wherein I feel the
touch of the Spirit.

I am passionate for the Spirit!

When I was a novice, in the first years of religious life, I had
profound spiritual experiences and feelings. It was like being in
love with the Divine! But, now that I'm getting older, I'm more
hardened, more wounded. Sometimes I'm not very aware of this
Spirit, but it remains always. It's my first love.

I think this spirituality comes before the option for the poor.
Because, when the poor don't respond to your initiative, when
they vote for a corrupt president—you still remain with that call,
with that profound conviction of life.

I call it the Divine Spirit that always seeks out life.

I believe this is pre-confessional, pre-political, pre-verbal.
You in your deepest identity with God. Now, I think it expresses
itself in confessional forms—you may call it the Holy Spirit, or
God the Father, or the following of the Poor Christ.

But, at this deepest level, we're all united. The true contemplatives, be they Buddhists or Christians or from African religions—ultimately, they all feel this force.

Clearly, this Spirit expresses itself and is proved in social commitment. Until it finds historical, political expression, this force remains ambiguous, even dangerous. That's why Christ said we have to love God and our neighbor. Love of neighbor proves the authenticity this Spirit, of our faith and our love of God.

ॐ ॐ ॐ

True spirituality always passes by the way of "the other"—especially the poor and oppressed. That is, I am the Samaritan, and the other is lying on the roadside. I am alive and the other is dead. I'm from the middle-class, and the other is exploited.

The other who is most other.

And when this Spirit, this faith is radical, it is disposed to martyrdom. That is, a true person of Spirit is disposed to give his or her life for Christ who is in the poor. The Latin American people are deeply "martyrial"—they have to confront death, which can bring the liberation from fear.

Father Josimo, who was assassinated, was my student and friend. Chico Mendes, murdered, was also my friend. So many colleagues and friends have fallen along the way, and they are resurrected by the action of God! By the action of the people!

This destiny is very profound.

I wouldn't be surprised if I was imprisoned, tortured, killed. Why? This is part and parcel of the logic of this way of spirituality and liberation alongside the poor.

This is not to romanticize suffering or death. Martyrdom is only justified in favor of life. Martyrdom is a consequence.It is dying against death to give life. It's the logic of Christ—and we must not separate the cross from a process of life for others.

Martyrdom is living for life so intensely that, well, the moment you have this disposition, you aren't afraid of anything.

One time in the Amazon we were raising awareness about the elections when the police surrounded us with machine guns and threw us in jail. We stayed the night, until the bishop intervened and freed us.

But, for that night in jail, no one was afraid. We prayed! We sang church songs! We gave cheers! Because when you have this conviction, this faith, this option, you have no more fear of death.

I don't know if I will come to this myself.

ఴ ఴ ఴ

Three years ago I had a profound breakdown from stress.
I had to interrupt my activity for some months.
My doctor made me relax and get exercise. Now, whenever I can, on Mondays I go fifty miles out of town to work manually in the fields. Tough work! With a hoe and pickax, planting trees, flowers and orchards.
This is beautiful. It's so good to be with nature!
You begin to love trees, love the land. You have different relationships—not only with ideas or persons, but with concrete reality. You begin to experience friendship with creatures. The stones begin to speak!
And your whole spirit benefits! You're more free, more light, open-eyed and wise—less musty and closed. You're more integrated in soul, body, spirit, mind.
I also do yoga and Tai Chi. I learned to drink tea in Japanese style, calmly, with serenity, without speaking about serious things.
This is all so essential to recuperate our humanity—to liberate what is most fine, most noble, most profound, most human within us. Life isn't only struggle. It's struggle and play! Work and dance—like the Greeks and Spartans who prepared for war with ceremonies of music and dance!
Five years ago we thought these things were bourgeois. Today we've rediscovered that they are good!

ఴ ఴ ఴ

*Writing and teaching in the line of liberation theology for so many years, where do you think liberation theology needs to grow?*

The first challenge, which I've been writing on lately, is the need to create a ministry to the masses who aren't organized. When these people elected Fernando Collar de Mello as Presi-

Clodovis playfully poses for a photograph reading a book by the "earlier" (less conservative) Cardinal Josef Ratzinger, prefect of the Sacred Congregation for the Doctrine of the Faith, the organ of the Roman curia responsible for the silencing of Leonardo Boff and other theologians.

dent,[†] we realized that the church of the base really wasn't present among the most marginalized masses at the periphery—the unemployed, the forty percent of Brazilian workers who earn less than a minimum wage [$45 a month].

The elections taught us that the church and liberation theology were more present among the organized people in the unions, grassroots movements and neighborhood associations who are only twenty percent of the Brazilian people. These people voted for Lula from the Workers' Party.

The CEBs in Brazil include roughly five percent of the Catholic population—perhaps ten percent in the more advanced dioceses. This community work hasn't valued the popular religiosity that is so important to reach the masses—Sunday mass, novenas, etc. So, we need a new ministry to the masses that retains a liberating content, but with a special methodology—a more emotive methodology, that draws on images and feelings.

The second challenge is on the opposite side of the CEBs—the ministry to the middle-class, another theme I'm working on.

Just as our abandonment of the masses gave space to the Pentecostal sects, our abandonment of ministry to the middle-class opened a space for the charismatic movements and the conservative movements like Opus Dei, Communion and Liberation, Tradition Family and Property. Why? Because the middle-class is restless and open, with good will.

The middle-class participates in the Workers' Party, the unions and the movements. They're even sympathetic to liberation theology—reading books, attending teach-ins. But when we find middle-class people who want to work for liberation, we insert them into the pre-existing CEBs and movements. We're behind in a more *specific* ministry to the middle- and upper-classes—in the vision of liberation, in the line of Medellín and Puebla. We need alternatives to the conservative movements.

---

[†]Fernando Collar de Mello won Brazil's 1989 elections by a small fraction against his runner-up, Luis Inacio "Lula" da Silva, the labor leader who helped create Brazil's Workers' Party in 1979. In 1992, President Collar was impeached on charges of corruption, a process spurred by massive peaceful public protests and a vigilant press.

*It seems that in the beginning liberation theology worked only with the categories of rich and poor. Yet in the U.S. many of us are trying to work with the middle-class.*

Exactly! Earlier, we were fascinated with the discovery of the poor. Everything was "the poor and the non-poor." As if there weren't other fundamental distinctions!

But, in the First and Second World, the middle-classes are not rich oppressors, even though they play the psychological game of the oppressors. There's a good portion who are open, who struggle, who sympathize with the oppressed. These are our allies. We can't turn them into adversaries!

*Is the ecological crisis also finding articulation within liberation theology? This seems to be a common ground of concern since it ultimately affects the whole planet.*

Our challenge is to elaborate this from the perspective of the poor. This will purify the vision of the First World, which is sometimes romantic—"preserving" nature. Our President and foreign banks are committed to ecology in a selfish way. They aren't interested in land reform, just their own profits. Our vision is one of *liberation*, of placing the environment at the service of the great majorities.

We need to start from an anthropocentric concept, because the creature should be cared for and saved—men, women, children, the Indian, the rubber-tapper, *within* their ecological context. We need an "eco-politics of liberation" that goes beyond simple romantic notions and class interests. It must be seen from the perspective of the poor, which is much more universalist.

*Hasn't Christian history often placed humans at the center to the detriment of nature, animals, creation?*

Yes, but I'd call this an "anthropo-monism," that is, man as king of the world. Ultimately, this is an "anthropo-dictatorship." An exaggeration. But careful! The other exaggeration is to put humans alongside bugs, butterflies, rivers. No!

After all, the Japanese banks, President Bush, President Collor de Mello are much more interested in preserving fresh air

than healthy children or Indians. When the Indians were massacred, they didn't do anything—they didn't react at all!

We need a certain hierarchy within the ecosystem. I don't
want to say that everything revolves around human beings.
Maybe "anthropocentric" is a dangerous word, but this shows
that we don't have an ecological vocabulary yet.

*Perhaps it's more helpful to look at the connections: We won't have
air to breathe if we don't defend the people who know how to protect the forest.*

Yes. And there's another challenge for us in liberation theology—the theology of *beauty*. Aesthetics. A European friend who
directed my dissertation said, "Clodovis, may I make a criticism
of liberation theology? It's missing fragrance." Enough said.

A bit more gratuity, beauty. The people have this! In the
poorest homes—flowers! Kind gestures of welcome! A desperately poor child will have a little ring on her finger! We have
to value beauty, which signals the transcendence of the human over necessity. This is very linked with ecology and with
the feminine.

*And yet the church has a poor historical record of valuing the
feminine.*

Do you know what I think? In the first place, the official
church, which is profoundly masculine, has to be reconciled with
the woman it carries within itself.

This church is very rigid, rationalist, powerful, self-secure,
arrogant. They aren't realized men with the courage of tenderness, the courage of life, of gratuity, of intuition, of the craziness
of the Holy Spirit! This whole feminine and human side is repressed inside them! So, clearly there's no space for women in
this church.

Now, the base church is very feminine. It's a church of
charism, vision, communion—feminine values. And the CEBs
owe much more to the presence of women religious who insert
themselves with the poor, visiting the families in their homes and
creating consciousness-raising groups, than they owe to the
priests who only come to say Mass and then hop in their car and
go to another community.

The root of the communities is very feminine. But at the level of representation, the community begins to "masculinize." This is a serious problem.

*Given the change in bishops and other interventions from Rome, do you have hope for the future of the CEBs?*

Hope? What a joke! These interventions will harm the CEBs, destabilize them, discourage many people, but it won't destroy them. No.

Look, there are two *big* reasons why they won't be destroyed. First, the CEB members are convinced that the CEBs come from the Bible. And the Latin American bishops supported them at Medellín and Puebla! Rome, Ratzinger and others won't destroy this deep conviction that brings us to struggle, even to death if necessary. The people say, "Even if our bishop doesn't want it, we'll still go forward, because we're with Jesus Christ and the Holy Spirit!" This is a legitimacy beyond all legality.

If you don't see this, it's because you don't live with the people. Even where the church tries to control the CEBs, like here in Rio, they're still around! Like trees in a big storm, the leaves fall and the trunk may even break, but the root is still protected. It is protected by the Holy Spirit! I have no doubt!

*What is at the root of this conflict between the church of liberation and Rome?*

The final root is the separation between the Vatican and the church at the base. The Vatican is very far away, physically and culturally! This separation from the people creates authoritarian and centralized structures. If the people at the Vatican were pastors and did ministry among the people, they'd have a different mentality.

*Would you want the Pope or Cardinal Ratzinger to spend time in a poor neighborhood?*

Ah—this is the only salvation!

If the Vatican only changed in that the Pope required his functionaries to have pastoral work in the periphery, with the people. Even in the city of Rome! There's tremendous poverty among the gypsies—40 million poor in the European community.

So, the first sin isn't Ratzinger's or the non-democratic authority machine. The foremost defect is that this machine is removed from the people, from the bases. Heed this: the Roman curia is removed from its main body, which is the Third World. Nearly fifty percent of all Catholics are in Latin America! And the center of the church is still hooked solely into the First World! They're under the influence of a consumeristic ideology of a "happy" capitalism. But it isn't "happy" for the rest of the world.

*Have you had problems with the Vatican similar to your brother Leonardo's silencing?*

No. I'm not a theologian who reflects on the macro structure of the church, like Leonardo did in *Church: Charism and Power.* I'm more at the micro level—the walk of the CEBs, grassroots ministry. This work is more immune to Vatican interventions because it's less visible, less public.

But I've had my own problems. For example, I was a professor at the Pontifical University of Rio [PUC] and the Cardinal [Eugenio Sales] withdrew my license. He even broke church law, which provides a process for withdrawing someone's canonical credentials. My superior general started a process in Rome against the Cardinal to annul this act, but it's not yet resolved. Meanwhile, I can't teach there.

Then my Superior General invited me to give classes in Rome, and Rome intervened and prevented me from teaching because they said my case still wasn't decided. It's been five years and there's still no resolution.

*Has that been painful or frustrating for you?*

No! The work with the people is very big! The fields are large and the workers few! The Reign of God isn't an order that comes from the hierarchy. The real life of the church goes beyond power schemes! It goes to the base, there where the people pray, where they gather together and hope for a new society. This is like throwing a bucket of water into a glass—it catches a little water, but the rest spills beyond it!

*In a small book called* A Way Forward for First World Churches, *you called Pope John Paul II a "catalyst of prophetic impulses." Do you still believe this description is true?*

I'm a bit more realistic lately! Before, I believed that the main line of the official church and the Pope was basically on the side of the poor. Lately, I see it's not. It incorporates the option for the poor, but this isn't the axis. I think the central pivot of the official church is the re-vitalization of religion in the modern person, the confronting of secularism. The question of justice and the poor is marginal.

The basic posture of the Pope is authoritarian—loving, benevolent, defending the poor—but still very authoritarian.

*You've written books and articles on the option for the poor. How would a person of privilege make that option?*

That depends. If we're talking about an oppressor—a large landowner, a banker, an industrialist—this means a really profound conversion, a radical transformation of his or her existence. Because it is not possible for a rich person, as a rich person, to be a Christian unless he puts his riches, his position, his strength at the service of the poor—which is extremely rare. It's like a personal death.

As for the middle-class, normally they don't have such a firm class position, they blow with the wind, revolutionary or reactionary. The option for the poor demands a decision, a definition of class. It doesn't matter what class or profession you are. The important thing is what side you're on, in what direction do you put your strength *as* a professor, a doctor, a land owner, a businessperson.

*So what might solidarity with the poor look like for these middle-class people?*

Concretely, it's an option for life. For example, you can struggle for a transformation of society, join political groups that are committed to change, educate your children with a sense of justice and love for the poor. The important thing is that core option. Specific solidarity comes later—presence with the poor, financial assistance to groups seeking change, putting your profession competence at the service of the poorer classes, at the service of the causes of justice.

We need a lot of creativity! Maybe it even starts with our lifestyle—this consumerist, addictive, accommodated lifestyle. Maybe we start by living more modestly, with sobriety, in evangelical poverty. But the important thing is the reason why. If you have a reason why, you'll find something to do.


*Like you said earlier, liberation theology needs to work with the middle-class, who are born bourgeois just like the poor are born poor.*

We liberation theologians and bishops suffer from this! All of our bishops who were converted reveal a secret: they were converted through direct relationships with poor persons.

It's difficult for rich person to convert only on a retreat or reading a book! This can open you, but the act of conversion comes when you enter into contact with black people who live in the *favela*, with women domestic servants, with strangers. Living, organic, physical contact with your skin. We have a very rationalist idea of conversion—it's in the head. But it passes through the body! The body becomes aware!

If you're always in the middle-class, middle-class friends, middle-class neighborhood, middle-class parish, middle-class school, there's no real way to break with it, even if you have good ideas and intentions. You start little projects to *donate* to the poor, but you don't make a deep option for life.

You'll only have a conversion when you break with your world and have contact with the poor. Like St. Francis who kissed the leper. You must kiss the leper.


*So, someone from the middle-class in the U.S. who wants to help this process might facilitate personal encounters, be a bridge.*

Exactly! This is essential. To be a bridge.

Like I said, Rome will only have an internal revolution the day it physically "third-worldizes" itself. The Pope would be a lot worse if he never visited the Third World! After visiting the Third World, he opens up a little bit. To the extent that he touches the reality of the Indian, blacks, the poor.

The crucial function of a ministry to the middle-class is to put them in contact with the poor. Only there do you establish true solidarity. Not necessarily permanent contact, but sustained contact. Every weekend, every two weeks, for a month, a semester. Not paternalistic, but building friendships. Working *with* not *for* people.

*What message of solidarity would you like to offer to people outside of Brazil?*

I think we live in a global village. The world is smaller every day. You are here speaking Portuguese. Leonardo just returned from Europe. We're all neighbors!

So, we need to get to know each other better. We need a new kind of pastoral tourism—a solidarity vacation! Groups come from Italy to visit our CEBs and take advantage of our beaches as well. We give courses abroad and share our experiences.

The U.S. will never be a free and happy nation while they continue to exploit and marginalize the Third World. The Third World will never be happy or free so long as there is a First World stuck in the mire of consumerism, alienation, indifference.

We are alienated by misery. You are alienated by opulence. But we're both alienated—you by luxury, we by the pain of abandonment! And we can't be liberated alone. Like Dom Helder said, "We are liberated together, or we are alienated together."

*In other words, my liberation is linked to the liberation of the poor?*

Exactly! Intertwined. You help to liberate us from basic material needs, but we help you become liberated spiritually. Morally! The poor give the hope of utopia, they bring the dream to humanity.

The First World doesn't have a dream. It doesn't think about a new, alternative future. It only conserves, protects, accumulates. The sad thing about Eastern Europe is that it wants to enter the same road as Western Europe and America, nothing new! It doesn't want an alternative society, which would be neither bureaucratic socialism or consumeristic capitalism.

We need this mutual solidarity.

# 12

## LEONARDO BOFF

I see more and more each day that every person is the bearer of a great human experience—the popcorn vendor, the trash collector, the person who sells French fries on the corner.

If you really converse with people, you can learn so much! So much wisdom, so much suffering.

*Leonardo Boff is perhaps the most published and certainly the most publicized Latin American liberation theologian. The Vatican silenced Leonardo from May 1985 until March of 1986 in response to his book,* Church: Charism and Power. *The silencing guaranteed him a far broader hearing than he ever imagined.*

*I interviewed him in the fall of 1990, a year and a half before he left the Franciscan priesthood to pursue his writing and teaching free from church intervention. Boff explained this decision in his letter of resignation, "I am leaving the priesthood, not the church. I am leaving the Franciscan Order but not the loving and fraternal dream of St. Francis of Assisi. I am and will always be a theologian who is Catholic and ecumenical, coming from the poor, opposed to their poverty and in favor of their liberation."*

*At the time I interviewed him, he was teaching theology at the Franciscan Major Seminary in Petropolis. (The Franciscan Prior later ordered him to stop teaching.) The mountainous ride from Rio to Petropolis is breathtaking, and the city itself reminds me of an Alpine village. Yet the grinding poverty of the favela is not far away. For many years Leonardo Boff assisted the CEBs in the*

Leonardo Boff stands in front of a statue of Francis of Assisi in the courtyard of the Sacred Heart of Jesus Franciscan Monastery, where he lived as a Franciscan priest.

*"Favela do Lixo" (literally, "favela of trash," where people re-sell bits of trash to make a living.) The participative style of the CEBs figures prominently in Leonardo's controversial books.*

*Today, Leonardo is a professor of ethics at the Rio de Janeiro University. Leonardo is still active in the defense of human rights, unions, the land movement and housing cooperatives; and he is a resource person for the CEBs at a national level.*

*Leonardo escorted me to a front room in the beautiful Franciscan Sacred Heart of Jesus Monastery, his home at the time, and generously shared three hours with me. We each grew more and more animated as we danced through topics of interest to us both—mysticism, spirituality, world religions. Through it all, he guffawed at Rome's folly, and grieved Rome's betrayal of the poor.*

શ શ શ

My grandparents were born in Northern Italy.

At the end of the nineteenth century, they moved to the south of Brazil, Rio Grande do Sul. My parents are now Brazilian, but we spoke Italian at home until I was ten.

I entered the Franciscan seminary when I was eleven, but my true conversion wasn't my becoming a religious and a priest! These were natural decisions given that my family was very religious.

My real conversion to theology wasn't until 1970. This occurred just after I returned from Europe, where I studied with the great European theologians—Johann Baptist Metz, Karl Rahner and others. I was invited to preach a retreat in Manaus, the principal city in the Amazon, for missionaries coming from the interior of the jungle. Some traveled a week on boat, others spent a month en route.

When I arrived there I realized that my progressive, European theology had very little to say to them!

It reached the point where I had a psychological crisis and became mute! I couldn't speak because of a stiff neck and sore throat. I thought, "These people traveled a week or more to hear the current Christian message—and they won't find it!"

My theology was inadequate.

I realized then that theology had to start with the challenges of poverty and misery. You see, almost all of those retreatants were from Canada, Italy and the U.S. They left their homelands

In a typical favela, such as this one in São Paulo, the city offers no public sanitation service. People are often seen sweeping trash out of the dirt ravines in front of their homes.

to live in the rainforest as a gesture of generosity and identifica
tion with the poor.

Theology would have to start with their questions.

ఴఴ ఴఴ ఴఴ

So, after that, I began to enter the reality of our Brazil.

In 1971, realizing that theology had to be marked by a social
liberating dimension against oppression, I wrote *Jesus Christ Liberator*. This work was the fruit of my crisis, the fruit of this encounter between the challenges of reality and faith in Jesus.

This is what liberation theology is—the effort to reclaim and
develop the political dimension of Gospel faith in order to reinforce the struggle of the poor. The poor were the first subscribers
of the Gospel. Jesus became poor.

Until now, the political dimension of Christianity has reinforced the established powers. The bishop was always allied with
the governor, mayor and other authorities.

The core of liberation theology is profoundly "theologal"—
that is, rooted in the very nature of God. You see, there's an immediate relationship between God, oppression, liberation: God is
in the poor who cry out. And God is the one who listens to the
cry and liberates, so that the poor no longer need to cry out.

I tend more and more to use the category of "the one who
cries out" rather than "the poor." Everyone cries out. A woman
starting a new life, a marginalized black woman, a child who
can't go to school because of hunger—they're all crying out!

My question is: Who listens to the cry of the poor, to the cry
of women, the cry of those who are suffering?

Liberation theology is born from this effort to listen to the cry
of the oppressed—even the rich person who cries out because
they're in despair! The person who suffers from an empty life
must also be liberated and listened to. God also listens to them!
Jesus cried from the cross and God resurrected him.

It is only passing through the cross, through the crying out,
that God can say, "Everything is going to be OK."

ఴఴ ఴఴ ఴఴ

For years I've been working on the theme of the Holy Spirit.
On the level of spirituality, I think our vision is too human-
centered. It's even very Christo-centric.

I think there's a dictatorship of Christ in Christianity!

We also have the Holy Spirit! And the Spirit doesn't only repeat what Christ said and did. The Spirit is open to what is new.

The Holy Spirit also helps us see that we can come to God through the experiences of all the great religions. We should never speak of "anonymous Christians."[†] This is another form of Christian imperialism! Nor should we speak of the "third millennium"—this is Christian discourse, the language of the victors. The Jews have been here a long time—and the Buddhists are in their sixth millennium!

I think we have to have, let's say, a house, a home. Each one is born into a family and lives there. I would say, "I'm Catholic."

Now, I'm not dogmatic or confessional. *As* a Catholic I relate with Protestants, the Orthodox, Macumba[††] and Eastern mysticism. I appreciate the project of each one. They are not "anonymous Christians"—no! They are also bearers of the Spirit!

༆ ༆ ༆

I think this theology is undergirded by the belief that God doesn't discriminate or make exceptions for people. God communicates Godself in all of God's children, each in their own way. God even sleeps in the rock. Why not?

People say that God is a masculine adult who thinks. This is a *machista* view!

A child says, "God plays." God is in the child.

My perspective today is that we should re-think the theme of God—God as a child, a young person, an old person. God dreams in plants and in animals. Religion, then, becomes much more human. Every space is inhabited by God! Theologically, this is panentheism—God in all things. Not that all things are God, but God is in all things. There's a difference between panentheism and pantheism. We need to rescue this.

In this view, everything is central—not only people, but the whole Gaia—a great living organism with its own atmosphere

---

[†]The "anonymous Christian" approach to religious pluralism, identified with Karl Rahner (with whom Leonardo Boff studied) holds that people of non-Christian religions are saved by the grace of Christ when they live according to authentic human values.

[††]Macumba is an Afro-Brazilian ceremony with Christian influences accompanied by song, dance and drums.

and breath. The Spirit permeates people and animals, but also the rock. The rock also feels, grows—God's sleeping there, but is still present.

Why can't we think of God as one who is sleeping? There are theological reasons for this. Jesus was God and was a little baby who slept at times—God sleeping, feeling, dreaming!

At the core, there's a strong theology of life here in Latin America, a theology not only of the life of the poor, but everything that deserves to live. There is an immense cosmic democracy!

This instills in us an attitude of respect—respect for the rock, water, plants. In a theological perspective, these are our sisters and brothers. We come from the same Creator. We come from the same substance of earth and share the same destiny.

Ecology itself exists within us.

All of nature dwells within us—the sun, moon, waters are all inside us as archetypes. For example, the moon is the symbol of intimacy. These symbols help us understand human beings more profoundly—less in terms of productivity, more in terms of gratuity, integrated with nature, belonging to a very broad circle of life.

やる やる やる

The Holy Spirit helps us understand God as absolute passion. Not as supreme being, but absolute love, life and passion that spills in all directions.

In this light, the Holy Spirit is the best expression of the face of God.

I hope the church changes in accord with this vision of God. This is the church I would like to see in the future:

First, a church that values every religious experience of humanity as a manifestation of God, since God visits all of God's sons and daughters.

Secondly, I'd like a church that values all manifestations of the legacy of Jesus, that is, Orthodox churches, Lutheran churches—the thousand forms of churches. All of them share in the inheritance of Jesus.

Third, I'd like to see an inclusive church. It would be a church that integrates women, men, children, old people, persons with AIDS, sick people, healthy people. It would be a space where human beings could experience inclusion without taboos, exclusions, or scapegoats.

This would be a non-hierarchical church.

It would need coordination, because not everyone can do everything. And we would need to serve especially those who can't do for themselves—the blind, the sick, people with AIDS, those that nature cheated.

Above all, it would be a church that didn't think only about itself, but would live as a great service to the religious experience of humanity.

Each and every human has something of the divine in them. The face of every man and woman is the image and likeness of God! This church would allow people to express themselves freely—even when they make mistakes.

ᛦᚦ ᛦᚦ ᛦᚦ

Personally, there are times I need to just get away. Relax. Disappear.

The very discipline of writing demands solitude. Sometimes I even need to hide myself, so I go to a friend's place outside of Rio. I stay for a week enjoying my solitude.

I may spend ten minutes only feeling the heat, or cold, or the wind. Or I listen to the multitude of sounds then try to hear my own heartbeat.

But, I also like being in the midst of the people!

Unfortunately, when I am with theologians I feel like everyone is disputing with one another, seeing who has the better arguments, who is more articulate.

I don't feel comfortable in this atmosphere.

I see more and more each day that every person is the bearer of a great human experience—the popcorn vendor, the trash collector, the person who sells French fries on the corner.

If you really converse with people, you can learn so much! So much wisdom, so much suffering.

Theology alone doesn't convince anyone.

Only those words which are pregnant with action, theology that is born of suffering, of struggles, of the poor—this theology is a testimony. This theology leads to conversion.

ᛦᚦ ᛦᚦ ᛦᚦ

*In your own work and that of other theologians, what directions would you like to see liberation theology go in the future?*

First, I think we've really neglected the question of culture. In the past we addressed politics and economics, but we missed other profound dimensions of human beings. Today we understand that every human group is mediated through culture—black cultures, poor cultures, cultures of silence, of the oppressed, of women. Liberation will only be authentic if it creates its culture—its symbols, songs, elaborations, discourse.

Secondly, I would criticize liberation theology for not yet listening sufficiently to the poor. Our theology is for the poor, not of the poor. Nor is it a theology directed towards the poor! We still use the discourse of First World European theologians. I think the struggle, the suffering, the legends of the poor, the way they speak, their life experiences—this should all enter much more into our theology.

Thirdly, we're trying to develop a "pastoral of the allies"—a ministry of the middle class. We have ministries for the poor, Indians, peasants—but what do we do with the middle-class? They're very important in the process of change because they control public opinion and have the freedom that modern culture and their economic position gives them. We should do justice to the middle class. They can be Christian as middle class people but *allies* with the poor, not allied with the class above them that they usually imitate. The question is how to help the middle-class reflect on their experience and opt for the poor.

*Some say that CEBs aren't possible among the middle-class. But middle-class groups do organize around the life and death issues of militarism and ecological destruction. Don't you think these are also "base communities" because they're struggling for life?*

Yes, and these global issues also affect the poor! The poor don't have cultural or political conditions to think about these issues.

Artist Cerezo Barredo, a Spanish-born Claretian who lives in Latin America, painted this mural in the rural community of São Felix do Araguaia (in the central Brazilian state of Mato Grosso). Above the simple church altar, the image celebrates the CEB as the people of God guided by the Holy Spirit, symbolized by the dove. The words at the upper right proclaim, "In the liberty of the children of God."

I think that middle-class communities, if they're in *communion* with grassroots communities among the poor, have an important function. Perhaps they can even help Rome understand the problem of the poor! Rome doesn't understand because it doesn't have *experience*, it only sees the poor as one who doesn't have anything, as ignorant. Perhaps the middle class could be a *mediator* for the poor.

*Being home to the Amazon and to liberation theology, do you believe that Brazil has a unique role in articulating the issue of ecology in a theological framework?*

Brazil has an important role for two reasons. First, the Amazon is a global issue, and second, the Amazon isn't empty—it's inhabited by Indians! And the Indians are threatened with extinction. We discover among them the value of a people of God who have their own language and world vision, a way of being human that integrates men and women, people and nature. These values teach us how to live more richly as human beings. They also show us how to live in the tropical rainforest and extract resources without damaging the ecosystem. We can be friends to nature.

In Latin America, our key contribution is to assert that the first ecological aggression is misery. Poverty is the most dangerous thing for the environment because poor persons pollute water and take down trees just to survive.

*What sustains you personally amidst the continual criticism, censure and other interventions from the Vatican, including the year of silence you endured?*

Two things. First, at the personal level, I never felt these persecutions bothered me very much because they don't touch the deep convictions of my theology. I feel more the victim of injustice, of the arrogance and ignorance of the institution. Rome doesn't work with the truth of my texts. I often reject the positions they attribute to me! I am bothered more by these two attitudes of doctrinal jurisdiction—the mediocrity of their formulations and the arrogance of those who "hold the truth."

I've repeatedly claimed a thesis which, for normal theology, is heretical. I make the "heretical" affirmation that the Holy Spirit became incarnate in Mary. Thus, we can adore Mary just as we adore Jesus. I've published this twice and Rome doesn't say anything. This is a profound theological question: What is the eschatalogical vision of women? Are women also invited to be bearers of divinity? But if I say half a sentence from time to time about the Pope not being infallible, then they criticize me, because this touches the inside of the church!

I also say that Jesus was not a unique, not the only incarnated one. Rather, he is the first among many brothers and sisters. Every human being will be assumed by their own Eternal Word and be like Christ in their own way. I published this in many books and Rome never said anything, yet these are hotly debated issues! Traditional theology says the incarnation was a singular event—only Jesus, not us.

What really sustains me in these trials is my contact with the communities, the people, who say that all of these questions from the hierarchy are peripheral, that the church doesn't understand the struggle of the poor or the theologians who struggle alongside the poor. Many times the people pray even for Cardinal Ratzinger, that he better understand our position. They pray that the Pope will always defend the poor.

This gives me peace of mind. This makes me certain that, for me, the criteria of the poor is truly infallible, and not the criteria of the Holy Office.

*What's at the core of this conflict between the Vatican and liberation theology?*

At the roots, this is a conflict of power in the church: Who rules and what are the means of participation.

The grassroots of the church in Latin America, also in the U.S. and Africa, are becoming aware that they *are* the church, not merely customers. So they're participating in liturgy and ministry and all of the sudden they say, "We want to participate in the decisions of the church as well!" Then the powers-that-be say, "You can't because you are not priests. The bishops and priests decide in the church!"

The traditional theology of Rome says that the clerical institution is the well of Christ and is thus untouchable. So the clerical body retains all power in the church and administers this power "for" the lay people, never "with" the people. And the people don't have the right to their own ecclesial projects and dreams! They have to dream what the clerics dream.

Along with this is a theological problem. I believe that Rome is afraid of God—afraid of the free God of the poor, a Trinitarian God. The model of the Trinity allows the church, in fidelity to itself, to incorporate the people and adopt a democratic, participative way of being. For me, this crisis of fear will decide if the church is going to be a fortification of authoritarianism, *machismo* and exclusivism, or if it will be a church open to women, laity and the poor.

Now, for the past thirty years a certain journey has profoundly transformed the Latin American church and the bishops. That is, the ecclesiastical authorities who wield power have become pastors, walking with their people, suffering, persecuted, denounced, some killed. They earned a great moral authority alongside the people. They allowed themselves to be evangelized by the people.

Rome sees that this process is more and more irreversible. So either the whole church will begin to change in response to this journey, or this "heretical" process has to be sectioned off in order to preserve the institution as it is. So, for example, they condemned me and my book on the church as a "praxis that induces the people to act heretically." They don't analyze the doctrines, they only pay attention to the change in praxis, in participation, which can change the structure of the church. Ultimately, this is a problem of power.

*What do you mean when you say that the Vatican is afraid of God?*

First, when fear enters the picture, so does a lack of faith. The Bible poses that the opposite of faith isn't atheism nor the denial of God but fear.

I think they fear the true God of the Christian faith who is a Trinitarian God. They believe in a God of monotheism, of Judaism, of Islam, a one and only God, represented on the earth by Jesus, and Jesus is represented in the Pope. This is the God of political monotheism.

Now, when we say God is not one but three in communion, this means that *love* makes a God. The three dwell in the cosmos and wherever there is communion, participation and inclusion—there God is present. They're afraid of this!

This is why my book on the Holy Trinity could be the most political book I've written, because it touches the fundamental structure of patriarchy, Western authoritarianism and ecclesial clericalism. For me, a Trinitarian church would evangelize itself and open up, not because of natural reason or political pressure or even because of the experience of the poor! Rather, it would open up because it finds this theory to have the divine reason of revelation.

In other words, let's use the very weapons of faith, which are the theological weapons of the Trinity!

*With so many levels of attack—closing seminaries, silencing and firing theologians, nominating bishops—do you have hope for the future?*

On the one side, I'd say that Rome is committing what is, in my view, one of the gravest sins one can commit—killing the hope of the poor, of Christians that dream of a church of fraternity and solidarity. They are killing this hope.

On the other side, I believe this can cause a great conflict in the church as Christians create their own communities according to the Gospel. A more clerical Christianity will emerge, more and more distant from historical, political and social movements. And alongside this, not because the people want it, but because they have no other alternative, a marginal Christianity will evolve, with an evangelical, grassroots tenor. It will draw support from bishops here and there, but they will make their own way and may, slowly, be exorcised by Rome.

*Are you saying there could be a schism?*

Not a schism provoked by the people, but by Rome. Rome will say, "This is no longer the Catholic church." And they will say, "Yes, we are from the Roman Catholic church, and the Catholic

church is not only the Pope but a *great* tradition of the martyrs—
Romero, St. Francis, St. Ignatius—and we are in communion
with them."

I think this may be the *price* we will have to pay.

On the other hand, Rome should think hard about this—by
the year 2000 half of all Catholics will be in Latin America. If
Rome wants to maintain its institutional strength, it should listen to the peripheries of Asia, Latin America, Africa and the base
churches of the U.S., especially women. Women also make up
half of the church!

*Why hasn't a female theologian ever been silenced? Do you think
this, too, will come?*

No—they are already historically silenced! This is in the
Bible: women don't speak in the church. Rome considers women
in the world of silence, thus they don't need to silence a woman.
The challenge is for women to break the silence and speak.

Our evangelical conscience should lead us to struggle so that
women *can* speak because only women can give us a feminine
experience of God, of grace, of Christ. When we put women on
the periphery of the church, when we render them invisible and
silent we deny ourselves a way of knowing God that only they
can give!

The experience of women doesn't exist in the official discourse of the church, which is celibate, *machista*, patriarchal.
And unfortunately the church isn't overcoming these differences
but reproducing them—man/woman, cleric/non-cleric, inside/
outside—always dualist!

For me, this dualism betrays the utopia of Jesus. His dream
was to tear down all walls—between men and women, pagans
and Christians, the saved and the lost. All are welcome in the Father's house as sisters and brothers. I think we should struggle
so as not to lose the dream of Jesus!

*As a male liberation theologian are you afraid that you have to give
up some privilege so that women can speak?*

As men, we are the heirs and architects of domination. We
have forces within us that marginalize women. We have to strug-

gle against our very selves. It takes a certain humility to see the many things I do that are sexist, *machista* and patriarchal.

But the best way to struggle is to listen to women. Let them speak. And often, after so many centuries of silence, when she begins to speak, she cries out. This is a legitimate pedagogical process! Some call this exaggerated, but women have the right to shout after centuries and centuries of having to listen without being able to speak.

Personally, I still have much to learn and women are helping me. For me, this isn't a theoretical issue but profoundly practical—how do I live with women? How do I integrate the feminine in myself?

In fact, I think that if the church doesn't manage to overcome its problem with women, it won't be because of a deficient theology, but because the church hasn't lived with women, hasn't felt the skin of women, the tenderness, the capacity for friendship with women. It will be because people don't risk loving women simply by being human and vulnerable. It's pathological to view women as a temptation!

*Do you think a day will arrive that a theologian won't accept silencing or a bishop will just begin ordaining women?*

I have the impression that we will see a great drama of conscience: Whom do I obey more, the Pope or the people?

I think there will be prophetic bishops who say, "We are in theological communion with the Pope, who will be the symbol of unity, but we are not in juridical, canonical communion because we're in communion with the people, and the Pope does not listen." The Pope does not listen.

*You are posing this in such a way that it is not a rejection of Rome as much as a commitment to walk with the people.*

Exactly. And, with the people, demand that the Pope fulfill his mission of being the pastor of all people. If a schism occurs, it will come in this extreme crisis of conscience, with a Gospel tenor of *not* breaking away, not excluding. Schism usually happens when both sides exclude each other. Here, Rome excludes itself and walks away from the people. The people will not walk away from Rome.

*Is it a coincidence that the very church people criticized and scru-*
*tinized by Rome are often threatened or even killed by local eco-*
*nomic and military elites?*

I don't think there's an intentional agreement, but more a
harmony of structures. That is, the church lives in a regime of
*ecclesial* authoritarian security and the military elites live in a
regime of *national* authoritarian security. These structures produce the same kind of authoritarian people, with a super defen-
sive stance in their strategies and argumentation.

This is why they understand each other! They produce the
same discourse and attitudes—they don't need to meet to establish a pact. Their structural intentionality is the preservation
of the status quo: for the military, the status quo of capital; for
the church, the status quo of "symbolic capital," appropriated by
the clergy.

*Could a different pope change this situation?*

A change in popes won't do much. A pope linked to the journey of the poor and sensitive to social justice could give the Vatican a new orientation, but with the same difficulties Paul VI and
John XXIII encountered. We shouldn't ignore the actual nature
of the Roman Curia. Like a machine, Rome lives in profound
structural sin, and it no longer knows how to liberate itself from
this sin.

This is why Rome never understood the prophets—Oscar
Romero who was assassinated, Pedro Casaldáliga, Dom Hélder
Câmara or Cardinal Arns. It never understood liberation
theology! These are manifestations of the Spirit! Flesh understands flesh—power plays, security regimes, fortification
of clerical and authoritarian power, closed seminaries.
Everything revolves around security, never around freedom
of spirit.

The Spirit demands risk—the risk of error but also of cor-
recting oneself and learning from one's mistakes. The risk of in-
venting something that was never said in the past but that might
have the evangelical capacity to attract persons! They aren't capable of this.

*What have you learned from your own risks—especially the time and energy you have devoted to the poor?*

For those of us who come from the university, from the middle-class, poverty is a temptation for us to question God. How can we believe in God in the midst of such misery? And we blame God.

Not the poor. The poor person says, "If I didn't have God, how would I live?" God is the branch they cling to, the constant support giving meaning to their lives.

So, the poor teach us faith. They see God everywhere!

In spite of so much misery and political defeats, they always live dreaming that everything will turn out good. They have hope when hope is no longer a human virtue, when there's no reason for hope.

Also, the people have such love! Not bourgeois, subjective love—one person loving another. But love as solidarity, identification with the other. For example, a woman dies leaving five children and her neighbor adopts those children. They always do this! Without even knowing that this is the love of the Gospel! Nor do they call it a virtue—for them it's natural. In the midst of misery, they support one another.

This all makes me believe that the true temple of God is the world of the poor.

*Do you think this is romanticizing the poor?*

So many people speak of the poor as persons who lack something, but I say the poor *have* something. They have what we've lost and can't manage to recover.

There's a wealth of the poor and a poverty of the wealthy. That is, for the rich to maintain their privilege, they have to repress solidarity in order to exploit people through low wages. They have to forget that the other person is a human being with a family and children. They have to step on concrete realities: body, blood, compassion.

So, the oppressor is truly repressed. Their poverty is existential, often surrounded by an abundance of material goods.

I think we liberation theologians have stressed some positive dimensions of poverty, like the evangelizing potential of the poor. We have to recover the alternative character of the poor—they live an alternative culture, not by choice, but because they were thrown out of the system. I sometimes see that this great ethic is in the favela. There aren't assaults among them, no one invades another's property, they treat the children well. And there's a very religious perspective—God is always present.

The poor still sin, but they have a dignity that we often don't recognize. For example, I work in the "*favela* of trash," where the newspapers call the people "trash-pickers." The people don't like this and they insist, "No, we're not 'trash-pickers.' We are workers. I work to feed my children. I have dignity."

*Isn't it possible that a person will abandon this ethic when they cease to be poor?*

This is a pedagogical challenge to the churches of Brazil: for the poor to liberate themselves and keep their culture—their dance, their religion, their love of family—and to not become the victim of the dominant culture. This is very difficult because the equilibrium of forces is profoundly unequal. The dominant culture is tempting, offering higher salaries, the easy life, and many people are co-opted by this.

The way you reinforce this grassroots ethos is to reinforce the value of community. When one person stands alone, they're engulfed by the system; in community, you have a reference and can say, "I'd gain more money and have a profession, but I prefer the values of the community."

*Does it help when poor people see privileged people giving up comforts to stand in solidarity with them?*

Yes. Many intellectuals, doctors, lawyers and others are making the option for the poor by working in the periphery. These people take up this grassroots ethos. They identify with the poor, but the point is not for them to become poor. The poor don't want the rich to become poor because poverty isn't good! The people say, "We want the rich to walk with us, and place what they have—time, goods, science—at our service."

*So, there can be an interchange, each with something to share with the other?*

Yes, we call this an "exchange of wisdom." We give the wisdom of school and science, and the poor bring the wisdom of life, struggle, experience, and the wisdom of the tribulations of life. When these two wisdoms come together something really amazing happens!

The hardest thing for the poor is to believe they have value. They carry a mirror of the oppressor inside themselves. So, when they realize there are people from the dominant culture who stop being oppressors and become allies, companions on the journey, they discover that they have value. They discover that they can achieve so much when they organize—one weak person is weak, but two weak people are strong!

*If our solidarity with the poor liberates us from our "repression" can we then speak of a liberation theology for the First World?*

Yes. Liberation can't only be thought of in economic terms, but as a universal struggle where every human group has their own oppressions and crosses.

So, in the First World, people enter this hellish machine of accumulating things and end up forgetting their very selves, forgetting human relationships. But love can't be purchased! Fundamental dimensions of humanity are trampled on with a mono-culture of objects, of things to be consumed. I think one of the things that poor people teach us is how to live happily with few possessions.

What does it mean to be human? The First World has achieved the great ideals of the liberal, capitalist project—ideas rooted in the individual, such as accumulation and performance. You only need to see how people build houses—fenced in, with their own car, their own beach. Everything carried away by "my, my, my." But there's a great lack of intimacy, solidarity and basic community. There are conglomerates of individuals with no bonds between them. I think this brings oppression to the First World in the form of drugs, high levels of suicide, alcoholism, violence.

The other difficult thing in the First World is that in order to see the oppressions people have to do social analysis—analyz-

ing the economy, questioning government policies and multinational corporations. When you analyze these things statistically,
you'll see that the First World economies live from the de-
pendencies they create around their capitalist system—the
multinationals, investments, the political-cultural-ideological
systems of control, as well as the basic communication system.
Addressing this is the responsibility of Christians and other
critical citizens.

I believe that the fundamental task of First World churches
is to be pedagogical spaces of conscientization about the situation of the world, the globalization of problems and the relations
between countries today. They should also adopt a prophetic
voice to denounce the multinational corporations—their treat-
ment of the Amazon, low salaries, etc.


*Do you have a message for people in the U.S.?*

I have very little experience in the U.S., but the people I've
met are people of very *strong* solidarity. There's a sense of well-
being there, however, and most people don't see very clearly
who *pays* for this well-being, how the price is distributed
throughout the world.

To deepen your solidarity you must first discover within
yourselves, what are the oppressions that oppress you? Who is
crying out? From there, think of a strategy for listening to the
crying out and change things so that people won't need to cry
out.

There should be a liberation theology, not only from blacks,
not only from women, which are both important, but a liberation
theology from the U.S. as a whole. And not only from the U.S.,
Europe or Latin America, but today the issues confronting us are
global. We need a global response.

The second thing is to reinforce the bonds of solidarity
through information exchange and solidarity trips. If we have
more information, we can make better decisions in response
to the multinational companies and their destruction of the
Amazon. Who will listen to the cry of the poor in a political and
social way?

Before, socialism assumed this historical question and represented the proletarians of the world. The risk today is that with
the so-called overcoming of socialism, capitalism will not have an

ideological opponent or negotiation partner. In this new scene, who will listen to the cry of the oppressed?

Christians of good will should not stop listening to the cries of the world. We must propose a humanity of more solidarity. Interdependent rather than dependent.

# 13

# RUBEM ALVES

I say that the goal of our struggle for justice and all political struggles is for the world to be more beautiful. Poverty is horrid, it's ugly. Poverty is death, death of children, suffering. These are terrible things! They must end!

We live for beauty. The poets know this. I propose that instead of theology we do "theo-poetics."

*Rubem Alves is one of Latin America's best known Protestant theologians. His 1969 doctoral dissertation was originally titled* A Theology of Liberation, *but the publishers re-named it* A Theology of Human Hope.

*Rubem Alves studied at Brazil's Presbyterian Seminary in Campinas, then became the minister of a small congregation in Minas Gerais. He attended Union Theological Seminary in New York for advanced studies and was later invited to study at Princeton Theological Seminary in New Jersey, where he completed his doctoral studies.*

*Since 1974, Rubem has been a professor of philosophy at the State University of Campinas (UNICAMP), in the Brazilian state of São Paulo. In 1982, he published a widely acclaimed and controversial work,* Protestantism and Repression, *in which he critiqued the increasing conservatism of Brazil's Protestant churches. In recent years, he has devoted half of his time to his psychoanalytic practice and to the writing of children's books.*

*Before our interview, Rubem insisted on taking me to lunch at a local vegetarian restaurant. While walking through the woods on*

Rubem Alves sits in the garden behind his home
and work place.

*the way back to his office, he said with child-like enthusiasm, "Listen to the trees rubbing against one another! It's like they're making love!" The observation of a mystic and a poet—he is both. He champions the cause of "theo-poetics"—encouraging the use of poetry to express what scientific language cannot.*

*Rubem Alves is a man of buoyant spirits. He periodically interrupted our conversation to offer me a glass of wine or lead me outside to taste the cherry-like berries growing on the enormous* jabuticaba *tree in his back yard. Our juicy feast gave him the opportunity to explain to me the wisdom of the poor: "It was a poor peasant who taught me how to get the* jabuticaba *fruit off of the tall limbs—with a coffee can tacked on the end of a broomstick! We must not look down on the poor. They have so much to teach us."*

ஃ ஃ ஃ

I was born in a small, rural town in Minas Gerais in 1933. My father was once a rich man, but he went broke during the depression, which forced our family to move to the larger urban area of Rio de Janeiro.

I still long for rural life—the countryside, the old houses.

You know that crises are the occasion in which people are converted. Well, this crisis led us to the Protestant church. My father didn't have money to send his children to school, so the Presbyterian missionaries offered us the opportunity.

This was my beginning in Protestantism.

ஃ ஃ ஃ

I first wanted to become an engineer. Next, in utter admiration of Albert Schweitzer, I decided I would become a doctor and a musician. I tried to be a good pianist, but I didn't have talent. I was just like Salieri in the movie *Amadeus* who tried desperately to become close to Mozart. Like him, I just didn't have the grace!

Well, then I really changed. I was converted under the influence of a revivalist wave that came to Brazil during the 1950s. I

Rubem Alves not only takes great personal delight in nature but uses the imagery of gardening and the "Garden of Paradise" to speak in terms the Brazilian masses understand.

started seminary fully intending to become a Brazilian version of Billy Graham. But I was cured of this mortal disease!

Then I came to the seminary here in Campinas, which at the time was the center of creative thinking in the city and active with student and political movements. Your own Richard Shaull was a very important presence here.[†]

After studying theology in the Unites States, I came back to Brazil only to find that the church really didn't want me around! I was shunned for the kind of theological work I was doing. That's when I was offered a job as professor of philosophy in our State University of Campinas, where I've been ever since.

During recent years, much of my time is spent writing children's books, which I enjoy very much.

ᔰ ᔰ ᔰ

The most radical change in my life was the birth of my daughter Raquel in 1975. She was born fourteen years after the others—I felt like Abraham! When I was young I had strength but not patience. Later I had patience and wisdom, but no more strength.

Yes, Raquel's birth was a purifying experience in that it empowered me to say, "this is important," and the rest becomes blurred. Her birth re-integrated things in my life.

For example, when she was born I suddenly discovered that—absolutely—I would not spend another moment of my life writing academically.

I broke with the academic style because I decided that life is very short, very mysterious, and I didn't have the time to waste with academics. I would only say things in the most honest manner. If people like it, fine. If not, I can't help that. Today I couldn't write academically even if I wanted to!

This was a moment of true conversion.

I learned to tell stories for my daughter Raquel. I learned to write for children. There is a hospital nearby for children with cancer—conversations with my daughter about that brought me to write stories about death.

I have learned very, very much from all of my children. Without even knowing it, they have taught me about grace. They've

---

[†]Richard Shaull is one of the foremost North American Protestant interpreters of Latin American liberation theology.

taught me that education is useless! I've come to believe in guardian angels!

In other words, I don't raise my children. I can only hope that something inexplicable will happen, but it's not my doing. So when patients ask me how to raise children I say, "Leave your children in peace. The only thing you can do is be open and point out when they do something wrong, but always stand beside them."

૪ ૪ ૪

I don't know if the liberation theologians would consider me a liberation theologian. I don't consider myself one to the degree that I don't operate within Marxist categories.

Right now I get my inspiration not from sociologists, politicians or economists, but from poetry. For me, the classical, the traditional, the canonical, the socio-political mediation—these are heresy!

In other words, to speak sociologically and politically, I don't need to be a theologian, but a social scientist. If I need to send my car to the mechanic, I don't need to do theology for that, I just need science.

My understanding is that theology has to do with a dimension of experience that cannot be captured by scientific analysis. However, I don't reject scientific analysis.

I believe that theology is facing the abyss.

I must face the abyss, the abyss of existence, the abyss of mystery. There, I'm becoming mystical, you see? I have been reading the medieval mystics and oriental writers lately!

૪ ૪ ૪

I believe that the greatest problem facing us today is not the economic problem. The Brazilian people have an infinite capacity to suffer great deprivation *as long as* they believe they are building something beautiful.

But in Brazil, the people have lost hope.

With the loss of hope, we are no longer a people but a pulverized people. Like Augustine says in *The City of God*, the people are a gathering of persons united in love with a common vision and dream. Without this dream and vision, we are pulverized into fierce individualism, everyone defending their own turf.

In Brazil we are no longer a "people" because we don't have an utopia, a vision or a sense of hope. This is the crucial problem.

My own hope is mystical.

I am so deeply moved by the generosity of nature! When you ask me the greatest sign of hope, I feel like saying, "My *jabuticaba* tree!" Signs that appear in nature—after winter, after crisis, life miraculously appears anew!

And not just that. Hope doesn't even need these signs—it exists in spite of signs. There is a prayer in Habakkuk where the prophet says, "The fig tree is not flowering, there is no fruit on the vine, and yet . . . "

For me, this expression "and yet"—this is God. In spite of everything, we still have hope. This is the point of Paul Tillich's book, *The Courage to Be*—this courage that you have before life in spite of everything!

And there's Nietzsche. I would love to have lived 100 years ago to recover things from Nietzsche. His extraordinary study of Greek tragedies, where tragedy tears apart the hero and destroys everything. But in spite of everything, the hero continues celebrating life, life continues.

This celebration of life is beautiful and essential!

Even in the struggle for justice. I don't tolerate politics that come from anger. I want a politics derived from beauty.

The few really great warriors aren't those that come from anger, but from beauty. I only struggle well when I have visions of beauty. When the angry warrior kills the oppressor he's angry at, he will become very similar to the oppressor.

I don't admire politicians, but poets.

Like Gabriel Garcia Marquez. When I read *A Hundred Years of Solitude* and *Love in the Time of Cholera*, I think: if there is an all-powerful God, I would say that with this book, God is finishing the work of creation.

For me, the artists are our signs of hope.

They are the only ones who don't make a deal with death. There's a film called *The Seventh Seal* that ends in the dark ages when death leads everyone in a macabre death procession. There is only one who escapes the death dance—an artist. As the death procession passes by, he goes in the opposite direction. That's my point!

Scientific theology doesn't interest me because it's too linked with death. Analytic thought can be deadly.

ᛦ᛬ ᛦ᛬ ᛦ᛬

At times God is for me a wind, a cloud.

You might not understand, but images of love aren't fixed. Sometimes my image of Paradise is the garden in the back yard of the house I grew up in.

Jesus was born a little child. For me the image of God can be a father, a son, a friend. Other times God is a women, maybe a mother, maybe a granddaughter. Then there are times when I don't want God—I want a place.

In other words, God has a thousand names, a thousand images. I think it's blasphemous to have only one image of God.

I'd rather speak about experiences of the sacred.

These can be purely erotic experiences. They can be a variety of experiences—with people, nature, the forest, a flower, solitude. There's no single image associated with these experiences.

This is why I think it's heretical to write a theology. In the Bible you couldn't even say the *name* of God—now we are writing dissertations about God!

So I propose that instead of theology we do "theo-poetics."

The Soviet mystic Gurdjieff, a Russian orthodox and a great existentialist theologian, said "In Paradise there exists neither ethics nor politics, only aesthetics." Only delight. He concluded that justice is merely the means for the triumph of beauty.

I agree! I say that the goal of all political struggles, the goal of our struggle for justice is for the world to be more beautiful. Poverty is horrid, it's ugly. Poverty is death, the death of children. These are terrible things! They must end!

We live for beauty. The poets know this.

ᛦ᛬ ᛦ᛬ ᛦ᛬

*What do you mean when you say "there was no place for you in the church" when you returned from the U.S. to Brazil during the dictatorship?*

You see, the Protestants don't have a pope, so they don't have any authority that tells you to keep quiet. But there's a process of shunning—you become like a leper, you are never invited to anything. This is precisely what happened to me. Indeed, during the sixties and seventies I felt there was much more freedom

inside the Roman Catholic church than inside the Protestant churches!

A famous Catholic theologian once said that we Protestants don't know the meaning of papal infallibility. We saw it as an instrument of oppression. But really, papal infallibility was defined in such precise terms that everything outside this narrowly defined area was not infallible. On the other hand, we Protestants replaced this with "biblical infallibility," which is invoked by any pastor in any congregation, making the repression inside the Protestant church much worse than in the Catholic.

*You are no longer with the Presbyterian church. Do you still consider yourself a Protestant?*

Definitely. I am very much a Protestant—and this is why I broke off my relationships with the Protestant churches in Brazil. In 1970 I wrote a letter of resignation saying that Brazilian Protestant churches for me were a kind of grotesque resurrection of the most repulsive aspects of medieval Catholicism, and this was the reason why, in the name of Protestantism, I was resigning.

*Why do you think Pentecostal Protestant churches are flourishing so much in Brazil and the rest of Latin America?*

A sense of loneliness, the need for personal and emotional experience. One of the issues liberation theology has to face is that it has little to say about the personal dimension of life. If a father or mother comes with their dead child, it's no consolation to say, "In the future just society there will be no more deaths of this kind." This brings no comfort! The Pentecostals have a language for that, but liberation theology doesn't.

My feeling is that the liberation theology has to some extent unlearned the art of speaking directly to the very personal fears and anxieties—the fear of death, anxieties about the future, depression—because of its emphasis on sociological, political and economic criteria. As has often been written, the Pentecostals

Rubem swings underneath the *jabuticaba* tree in
his back yard garden.

don't pay due attention to the political. But, in my opinion, people choose a religion which brings them a word of consolation when they are facing personal tragedy, rather than choosing an ideology which promises overall social salvation.

*You strongly criticize liberation theology for its heavy use of the social sciences, yet you are a close and respectful friend of both Gustavo Gutiérrez and Leonardo Boff.*

Liberation theology is absolutely essential! In my version of liberation theology, which is born from an exuberant affirmation of the beauty of life, we are destined for this earth. For me, heaven is worse than the world! I hate heaven! I want the earth, these flowers, the *jabuticaba* tree! The origin of my liberation theology is an erotic exuberance for life. We need to struggle to restore this erotic exuberance, to share this with the whole world.

*I hear that you wrote a letter to Leonardo Boff on the occasion of his silencing. What was your message to him?*

Leonardo and I are very close friends. I wrote an article, a kind of personal meditation about his silencing, which I never dared to published. I said that for me, the vision of the Roman Catholic church is the image of the Gregorian chant. You see, the Gregorian chant has no sense of time. This represents the soul of the Roman Catholic church—there is no haste. So if one of the singers is silenced sometimes, it doesn't matter because the choir goes on singing! There is no sense of individuality.

My theory is this: these Catholic theologians remain silent because they simply cannot face the pain of having the mystical union with the mothers' womb cut off. They would rather keep quiet than be born into the uncertainties of the secular world!

We Protestants are a different kind of people because we are motherless. We are orphans, we are alone—you see? And, if we're alone, the only thing left for a motherless child to do is cry. So for Protestants the symbol is not the Gregorian chant, but the lonely prophet in the desert who cries out.

I ended my article by telling Leonardo how impossible his silencing was for me, saying, "Speak, Boff, Speak!" As you can imagine, I never got the article printed.

*What do you think is at the root of this conflict between the Vatican and the church of liberation in Brazil?*

For me it's very simple. Leonardo once told me, when he was under Vatican inquiry, that what was at stake was not liberation theology at all. I wrote an article saying that the Roman Catholic church can swallow liberation theology with ease! The trouble is ecclesiology. The question put to Boff was, "Why have you become a Protestant?" The trouble is the ecclesiology implied in the grassroots communities, it's a Protestant ecclesiology because it implies a transfer of authority from the Holy See to the local congregation. This is the heresy of Luther!

*Often the wealthy elites, military leaders and even death squads target the same people who are investigated by the Vatican. Is there more than just a coincidental link between these groups?*

Let me give a roundabout answer. About two years ago a São Paulo newspaper published a long article about a meeting of the representatives of the Latin American armies held in Uruguay.†† That document was amazing, because they listed all the dangerous theologians who should be kept under control. The list of theologians started with myself and also mentioned Hugo Assmann and Pablo Richard. None of the important liberation theologians were mentioned—not Gustavo Gutierrez, Clodovis or Leonardo Boff, or Frei Betto. I asked myself why. Surely the military couldn't be that stupid! And suddenly it dawned on me that the criteria for these lists were ecclesiological!

---

††The actual meeting of the 17th Conference of American Armies was held in Argentina in November 1987. It was later acknowledged by seven Latin American presidents at their summit meeting in Uruguay, in October of 1988. At the 1987 Conference, fifteen commanders-in-chief, including one from the United States, approved a secret continental security plan which was eventually leaked to the press by an Argentinean human rights lawyer. The document attacks liberation theology as a tool of international communism, and lists Alves and seven others as belonging to the most dangerous "hard-core Marxist" tendency in liberation theology. That category also included Salvadoran Jesuit Ignacio Ellacuría who was assassinated by the Salvadoran Armed Forces Atlatcatl Battalion in November 1989.

The military alone could not have devised that criterion for their selection. One group—those theologians who remained faithful to the church, who kept their vows of celibacy—were spared by the military because the Vatican watches over them. And the others—myself, a Protestant, and Hugo Assman and Pablo Richard, who were both married—were turned over to the secular arm.

At that point it became clear for me that there was a kind of coalition between military and ecclesiastical interests—as also occurred during the Inquisition.

*I heard you make a comment that when Leonardo Boff tries to go in new directions he has problems from both sides. Which sides?*

It's private judgment that, on the one hand, he has to face the Vatican. But, on the other hand, as a liberation theologian, there's an expectation that he'll go on speaking a certain kind of language. So if seemingly strange, more mystical dimensions appear in his writings, people don't always approve. For instance, I think his best books are on the sacramental life and on St. Francis. It seems to me that the liberation theology has no categories to assimilate both the themes and the style of these writings.

For me that main problem with liberation theology is not what it says, but how it says it. The truth is in the style.

*So how would you describe the style of most liberation theology?*

It's scientific, Cartesian. It implies an anthropology which ignores the unconscious. If it ignores the unconscious, I would say it ignores the Holy Spirit. If we are to believe Paul, the Holy Spirit abides in depths too deep for words. Personally, I think we still need to come to terms with Freud—not by accepting his conservative and reactionary political views, but by accepting his understanding of the unconscious.

I'd like to see us doing a theology that takes into consideration the unconscious. But the unconscious cannot emerge if the theology is Cartesian. If it's clear and distinct, there's no room for ambiguity! Medieval hermeneutics knew that the symbol has many meanings. The idea of one precise meaning, which is the essence of the scientific hermeneutics, is a Protestant creation.

Luther wrote about the "one single meaning" for the biblical text. But if you have one single meaning, whether from the conservative Vatican line or the progressive line, you must have inquisition—from the right or the left!

*I read an article where you describe "the theology of the kitchen." Explain what this means in the Brazilian context.*

The title of the article was "Living Room Theology and Kitchen Theology."[†††] In the living room we talk with one another according to certain rules of politeness about things that aren't embarrassing, things that we generally agree on. My hypothesis is that ecumenical theology, this conversation between Protestants and Catholics, has been a living room theology. Even when we argue, we do so according to a certain agreed-on etiquette which allows the dialogue to happen in the first place.

The kitchen is completely different. The kitchen is the place where unusual ideas visit us, where we don't think clearly, we think with our nose, our mouth, our senses. The German theologian Ludwig Feuerbach said that we are what we eat! This is a biblical view—the word is something edible, the sacrament is something we eat.

I am asking this ultimate question: What is an edible word? What does it mean to work with a word that isn't a thought but an entity to be absorbed into the body?

You see, in order to arrive in the kitchen, you have to pass through many secret places. In a Brazilian home, you have to pass through the places of love, the bedrooms. It is this very secret thing, which in psychological language we call the unconscious. This is the very thing that's absent in our theology! Ours is a theology of the conscious, that which everyone agrees on.

I am asking, what is a theology of the unconscious? This is my hypothesis: The political and ethical discourse developed by Protestants and Catholics alike represses the discourse of pleasure and love, the discourse of the kitchen.

---

[†††]In Portuguese, the living room is called the *sala de visitas*—literally, the room of visiting or visitors. Even in simple homes, the front door opens into this small room where guests are received. The kitchen is the room furthest away from the front door, and often opens into a tiny yard or garden, wash area and, further back, an outhouse.

It's significant that the Catholic bishops are divided on political issues—the bishops of the left and the right—but on sexual issues they reach an extraordinary agreement. For example, the Brazilian bishops of the left and right agreed to oppose the showing of the French film, "Hail Mary." When we speak of abortion and birth control, there's an amazing agreement, as if sexuality was the most crucial issue. Not one bishop would dare to doubt this or speak out!

It's like the story of Bluebeard who had a secret room that couldn't be opened. In both the Catholic and Protestant churches, there's a room that can't be opened. I believe this is the room of pleasure and sexuality. We've built an ethical and political discourse, but we've repressed the discourse of sexuality and pleasure.

*You frequently borrow images from everyday life and seem to have tremendous confidence in ordinary human beings. Where does this come from?*

For me this is linked with the psychoanalytic experience. In psychoanalysis, you have to abandon the idea of "fixing" people. You often don't know what to do! The only thing you can do is offer your companionship. That is, I can and want to hear your reality. The psychoanalyst believes that act of hearing the repressed reality of another person has a healing power, a power to restore human relationships.

I would say that one of the theological tasks is simply this: to *listen* to what the people are saying without attempting to fix it. What are the people saying?

*What else have you learned from your patients or from your friends who are poor?*

Even the patient in the worst situation knows that our relationship isn't just in one direction. To the extent that I allow myself, I am also being healed by them!

In relationship to the poor, it doesn't have anything to do with the Christian posture of generosity or the "preferential option for the poor." This is an ethical posture. For me personally, it is absolutely fun and fascinating to listen to what they have to say!

Why? For example, an illiterate person taught me how to get fruit from that *jabuticaba* tree. I've always done it the hard way! This person has wisdom—a way of knowing things, of conversing, a feel for time. Their way is completely different from mine!

I think the option for the poor is sort of arrogant, don't you? "I am the privileged one who will struggle for the poor. I'm on top and they're on bottom." I don't like this! They have something to say, and it is a true pleasure for me to listen.

*Don't you think it's important for people to struggle on behalf of the cause of the poor?*

First of all, I don't believe in the messianism of the poor. Poor persons suffer from the same struggles of selfishness as the middle-class. And we are all in need of God's saving grace.

Sometimes I wonder if there is so much virtue in "poverty." Every Biblical promise is against poverty—is of richness and overflowing. Nietzsche had a criteria for evaluating aesthetic creations: Is this creation a product of poverty or wealth? What's the difference? We see the difference in Blake, who writes about "wells overflowing." I think it is essential to restore without shame the beauty of the "overflowing."

So, for me, the important question for the worker or for the middle-class person is whether there is "overflowing." I am bourgeois. I work in the university, I have a car, I have a nice house, you and I just ate in a restaurant. I don't have to apologize to anyone. The essential issue is overflowing love.

If we believe in the theology of grace, we can't think that the overflowing love of God is restricted to the poor alone. The overflowing love of God is free.

*But doesn't this overflowing love have both a personal and a social dimension?*

Certainly, certainly. In specific historical situations I'd say that this overflowing is only expressed personally. Think of the mystics. There are situations when this love can't express itself physically. It's expressed literally like a great solitary song. Other times it's social. Look at the African Americans in the U.S. with Martin Luther King. Or look at the famous Brazilian demonstrations demanding direct elections! These were social situations of overflowing, where individual people felt like drops in a huge sea. Everyone singing, everyone feeling a part of a great movement.

*Do you write or speak about ecological issues in your recent work? Do these issues touch the Brazilian masses?*

Yes, I'm working on a book called *About the Political Garden.* The idea of politics comes from *polis* or the city. The classical city is the place where people can be human without being afraid. Inside there are beautiful spaces, gardens, and people. We've lost this. Our city today is a battle ground. We need this hope of a human space, a garden. The garden of paradise is a great symbol of harmony between humans and nature.

Once I was invited to speak at a conference of the CEBs. People were analyzing our social situation using classical frameworks, analyzing four hundred years of colonialism, repression, etc. Everything they said was historically and scientifically accurate. But the people there were housewives, poor workers, humble people from the periphery.

I began to speak about gardens and planting—practical things! The people all began to participate because everyone had this experience. This is the great difference between scientific theology, which works with concepts, and my theology or poetic theology, that works with images. Concepts speak to pure reason; images speak to the erotic. Let's say concepts are directed to the soul, but images are directed to the body.

What does this have to do with theology? When you speak poetically, you don't need to prove anything because the body already understands what you're saying! You refer to the gardens behind people's houses and say, "People don't want to transform the country into a garden." You make a bridge between the garden and politics through poetic language! So, poetry isn't just important "in addition to" everything else. It already is a form of direct communication—with the body, not just the head.

*Do you think that the historical Christian view of the body and nature has contributed to the exclusion and oppression of women?*

We must frame it in another way: The way we treat women is the way we treat men. Remember that Origen [third century] castrated himself! Why? It was an act against himself based on his concept of women. When you speak about oppression of women, you need to understand what men are doing to themselves.

I think Catholics are in a better situation than Protestants because the Catholics have the Virgin Mary. Protestants only have Mothers' Day! Catholics pursue a perfect mother in the heavens. They idealize the removed mother. You see this in children's stories—the mother is always dead and you have the godmother or stepmother. The Protestants have to deal with the empirical mother. She is alive.

I think both Protestants and Catholics have killed the woman for the sake of the mother. The whole sense of the virginity of Mary basically says "up with Mother, down with woman." That is, the church has a special place for the mother, but not for the woman; for maternity, but not for sexuality. Both Catholics and Protestants have enormous ideological structures that don't know what to do with the sexuality of women—or the sexuality of men!

*Having lived in both the U.S. and Brazil, which has more of a consumer society? And what function does consumerism serve?*

I believe that Brazil is more fascinated by consumerism than the U.S. Look at TV for instance. When I visit homes in the U.S., perhaps it because of who I visit, but the TV is very marginal. You turn it on to watch a specific program. But here in Brazil, TV has become the great shrine of the house! Family life happens around the TV.

Consumerism is part of capitalism—it's good business! Ironically, it functions to never allow people to become satisfied. The dialectic of our society is that of unhappiness. You consume because it promises you something. You buy something and the ephemeral promise soon becomes frustration—as soon as a new product appears. You are always trying to arrive at happiness, but you never get there.

*It seems we are all in the same boat—poor and rich, North and South—alike. How do we get out of this cycle of unhappiness?*

I don't know. I know a few isolated people who have broken with this lifestyle of consumption. This is very confusing to me,

because these more radical options of a simple lifestyle are possible for single people, priests. But there comes a time when you
realize you are a prisoner to a web of relationships. It is very difficult to make radical ruptures. It affects too many people.

*Do you see other options that are more available to people like you?*

Well, you can consciously reject money. For example, I spend
less time earning money so that I have more time to write or do
what I want. That is, I reject money or possessions because there
are other things I value more. Taking time to write is a disaster
from an economic point of view! You earn more money from one
lecture than from all the sales of one book. The question is what
is important to you. We have to commit to some things that are
absolutely insignificant in economic terms!

Members of Catholic religious communities are more privileged in this situation, which seems an injustice. The Catholics
have the luxury of Franciscan poverty! In reality this means
they don't have to worry about their expenses, illness or hospital bills, because the church and religious orders provide
everything.

# 14

# IVONE GEBARA

I live in a poor neighborhood in order to feel more directly the pains of the impoverished. This allows me to do theology in another way—trying to feel the meaning of being exploited in all ways. This closeness is also a constant invitation to struggle for a different world with at least minimal justice—the right to eat, to work, to live and love with dignity.

*Ivone Gebara, an Augustinian sister, is one of the most esteemed women theologians in all of Latin America. Her fields of expertise span theology, philosophy and anthropology. Ivone studied theology in São Paulo and received her doctorate in philosophy from the Louvain in Belgium in 1973. Returning to Brazil just a few years after the Medellín CELAM conference, Ivone chose to live and work in the destitute Northeast, in the town of Recife where Archbishop Dom Hélder Câmara was creating many opportunities for ministry with the poor.*

*Ivone taught theology, philosophy and anthropology at the Theology Institute of Recife (ITER), a creative and socially committed school inspired by Dom Hélder that trained seminarians and lay pastoral agents. She confides that she wept bitterly when the Vatican ordered ITER closed under the supervision of Bishop José Cardoso Sobrinho, who replaced Dom Hélder in 1989. Since then, Ivone continues teaching in an "underground" educational circle, as well as giving courses throughout Brazil and abroad. She also accompanies women's groups from various Christian churches, works with grassroots associations, assists in the formation of pastoral agents and has long participated in regional ecumenical groups.*

*Ivone generously agreed to meet me between two important appointments. She was heading to Rome with her religious congregation the next day. Pressed for time and anxious to begin, we met at the first place we found—an empty outdoor disco bar where the manager served us sodas, though they didn't officially open until evening.*

*Ivone's eyes sparkled with brilliance and the searching quality of a mystic. Passionate about philosophy, theology, anthropology and sociology, I observed how her life shared with the poor gives her a remarkable humility. More than any liberation theologian I have encountered, Ivone's work includes the voices of her neighbors—courageous and impoverished women living in the favelas.*

🍃 🍃 🍃

When I was a child, I was sensitive to the sick, beggars and outcasts. This fed my dream of becoming a doctor. But my parents, who were immigrants from Syria and Lebanon, believed that a woman's place is in the home.

I nevertheless insisted on studying and eventually chose philosophy.

🍃 🍃 🍃

When I was twenty-two I entered the convent—not so much because I was in love with God, but because I wanted to change the world. In fact, I experienced a strong crisis of atheism while studying philosophy. To this day, I have much sympathy for a certain type of atheism.

Being a nun was a way to hear a more beautiful music in the universe. A way to compose wonderful symphonies and create different relationships among persons.

Today, I live with a small community in a poor neighborhood in order to feel more directly the pains of the impoverished.

This allows me to do theology in another way—trying to feel the meaning of being exploited in all ways. This closeness is a constant invitation to struggle for a better world with at least

A *favela* not far from where Ivone Gebara lives in the periphery of Recife, Pernambuco, in Brazil's drought-stricken northeast.

.stice—the right to eat and work, to live and love with

/, I've learned more theology living in poor neighbor-
hoo⌣ .1an in classrooms. At times I wonder if the questions of
traditional theology have any meaning for the poor. And "the
poor" here means eighty percent of the population!

ঞ ঞ ঞ

It seems paradoxical that as a theologian I don't have an image of God!

If you want to call God love, as in St. John, I call God love.
But I don't have a fixed image. Rather, I feel encircled by the energy and mystery of life. I intuit that this universe, of which humanity is a small expression, is much greater than all the
theories about God, even Christian theories about God!

Prayer is being with myself in the presence of a greater mystery—but I don't know the name of this mystery!

I can call it God, but I'm afraid to speak of God, because immediately God is identified as the God of Christians, or Yahweh,
or God with a man's face and beard, the common image that I
also once held.

So I'm living through a very difficult period.

In the hardest moments of life I cry out, "God help me!"
But I don't know the face of the one who helps me. With this
cry, I'm gathering all of the human and cosmic forces, forces of
friendship.

I'm more likely to speak of God as Vital Force, Greater
Mystery, Love or Justice. I see God less as a being and more as
a value, an energy that dwells in us that I can't limit to a theory.

I need so much to pray.

I may read a text or let myself be swept up by classical music. Sometimes I pray in absolute silence, perhaps with a candle
that calls forth my interiority. Other times, I think of people I love
who are far away. Thinking of them makes me more understanding and enables me to love more.

And yet, when I am with the people, I pray the Our Father
and the Hail Mary—prayers they like to pray! Even these prayers
nourish me when I pray them in communion with the people.

I feel such a great passion for the world!

This passion is pure gift. I have no merit in it! This passion
sustains me in difficult times.

It strengthens me to see myself as part of this earth, neither more nor less, but part of it. I am seed, daughter, fruit, earth. This earth is my soul and my body.

ᢞ ᢞ ᢞ

In 1980 my eyes were really opened to the question of women.

For twelve years I was the only women on our interdisciplinary team. In 1980 I read two articles in a Concilium journal—one by Rosemary Ruether on the feminine image of God, and another by Dorothy Sölle called "Father, Barbaric Power." These two articles disturbed me terribly! They even began to affect my work with my colleagues.

Then I started working with groups of sisters. For ten years now I've been very troubled by the things that oppress nuns religiously—they come from men. Men are the ones who impose certain behaviors. The blaming of the body comes from them.

I also began to notice that while women at the grassroots level were submissive, their submission wasn't as strong at that of the women religious.

Then I saw that everything was connected. Even economic poverty is linked with a patriarchal organization of society. I began to link religion with economy, with society, with psychology—how women think of themselves as less than men. Why? Why do people say, "What a shame that I had a daughter and not a son!"?

Along these lines, I hope to offer a publication on Christology some day.

Somehow I feel that so long as we stick with a Christological framework that says God was incarnate especially in one man, which is the tradition—if we don't open this framework to see God present equally in man and woman, if we don't open our perceptions to the dimension of mystery in the revelation we call God, this force so much beyond us, if we don't open up beyond Jewish and Christian culture—then we'll just continue doing theology within the limits permitted by the institution.

But I don't have the wherewithal to develop this theme!

To write you have to have time and money.

I'm very busy, spending a lot of time with the people! Actually, I'm in a pretty tight situation. All of these groups—women in the poor neighborhoods, women religious, etc.—need facilitators, but don't have the means to pay them.

To write in these conditions is an act of heroism!

If you said to me today, "Ivone, stop doing everything so you can write," I wouldn't be able to. I need much time to write. I have a new booklet coming out, *Woman, Know Yourself,* but I wrote it by hand and typed it on a typewriter. The male theologians have computers, secretaries, etc.

Here in the Northeast we women who become theologians are few. Living in poor communities is important to us, but we also need the means to produce theology.

శ్రీ శ్రీ శ్రీ

When I do write theological works, I try to include the words and vision of poor persons. Their word is a critical word for me. How the poor—I prefer to say the impoverished—react, live, understand themselves is a critique of my theological theory. They say to me, "No, you're thinking isn't right." They balance my theory.

It's very difficult to be in both worlds. I think all we can ultimately do is build bridges. We can't fully assimilate.

Still, I would recommend that other theologians have more contact with impoverished persons. When we speak of theory, we need to know for whom we're speaking and of whom we're speaking. I'm never going to feel exactly what the poor feel, but I can draw near in sympathy, trying to feel what they feel.

శ్రీ శ్రీ శ్రీ

In my work I also speak and write about the body. People are sometimes shocked by this since I am a nun.

It's interesting, but I'm absolutely convinced that we do theology because of our body! My doctoral director, Rubem Alves, says that everything begins with the body. I thought about this and began to see that all oppression is an oppression of our bodies. For example, what is cultural oppression except for an oppression of the bodies of persons—bodies of production, the organization of bodies?

And Catholic theology has violated woman's body.

For example, burdening woman's body as sin or reading the Bible and the "virgin" birth of Jesus as a way of despising the reality of nature.

I react to this and present another reading.

I speak of the importance of a virgin body, but a virgin body isn't virginal because it's free of sexual contact. It's a virgin body because it's not an idolatrous body. A body is virgin if it doesn't sell out to injustice.

It's the body that wants to build a just society. It's ethically virgin—which is more important than physically.

I try to read Mary, the mother of Jesus, as a symbol not only of women, but of humanity searching for ethical virginity. That is, not bonding itself with the destructive forces of the world. A woman with ten children can be an ethical virgin!

So, it doesn't matter if Mary was a biological virgin. She was a woman like any other woman. The virginity she represents is ethical virginity.

૪૭ ૪૭ ૪૭

*Do you consider yourself a liberation theologian?*

There is a "masculinist" Latin American liberation theology. I don't say *machista*, because I don't think they're *machista* in the pejorative sense. But I call them masculinist, and I'm more of a feminist theologian of liberation.

*What direction would you like to see liberation theology take in the coming years?*

From a feminist perspective, first, we need to keep working on the anthropological vision of liberation theology. There have been some steps by Gustavo Gutiérrez, José Comblin, Leonardo Boff, Jon Sobrino. But, their anthropological perspective is male-centered. They include women, but women are never the starting point. They don't start with the reality of man and woman or woman and man.

Secondly, Latin American liberation theology is done absolutely within the limits of the Catholic tradition, which is

fundamentally male-centered. People don't break with this tradition, because to do so they'd have to touch upon things like
power—power exercised by priests, bishops, the Pope. And
touching this power is dangerous. I have a feeling it's not going
to be the men who touch it, but the women.

Thirdly, liberation theology still hasn't developed much in
the area of cultural diversity. This is because the poverty in Latin
America is so dramatic—the contrast of poverty in a continent
that has the means to feed its whole population! So liberation
theologians focused on economic analysis, which is essential.
But we need to open to other horizons.

*As a feminist liberation theologian, how would you describe the
development of feminist theology in Brazil?*

I feel that here in Brazil and Latin America, feminist theologians want to open a space inside of patriarchal theology. That
is, they criticize patriarchal theology, but they use the very same
principles and dogmatic formulas. They use the Bible, looking for
the place of women, but their hermeneutic is still fundamentally
androcentric. They criticize patriarchy, but keep using the name
God Father, Father, Father.

What would the alternative be? To produce a new theology
that doesn't fear discord with the tradition. When I read the few
texts of Latin American women theologians, I see their *fear* of
saying things that differ from the tradition. Even I have this fear!
But in my heart, in my body, in my inner being, I beg to speak
differently!

*Are you familiar with U.S. feminist theology, and, if so, do you
think U.S. and Latin American feminists have mutual insights to
offer each other?*

I feel an affinity for U.S. feminists like Elizabeth Schüssler
Fiorenza, Rosemary Ruether, Letty Russell, and I like the first
phase of Mary Daly. But I think we still lack a mutual exchange
between us. They probably read a little of our work, but we

A rural woman worker in the fields of northeast
Brazil.

produce very little, which is a serious problem. They have much greater means of producing feminist theology.

While I've learned so much from them, I also think we have much to contribute. That is, feminist theology, especially in North America, is very advanced theologically. But here we have much contact with impoverished women, whose feminism is framed differently. For example, in reality, poor women don't have my feminism. They have another kind of feminism—that is, without any theoretical discussion, they act as heads of families, making family decisions. I'm saying this in general, because there are still many who are absolutely oppressed, beaten, raped.

But, I call theirs the "feminism of poor matriarchs"—the feminism of survival, the feminism of the Afro-Brazilian religions, such as Candomblé, where the women have a spiritual authority that has nothing to do with the authority bestowed by Catholicism. This is a diverse, feminist world without calling itself "feminist."

I think there's much to gain if we had the opportunity to dialogue with North American feminists. We would help them to recognize the feminism of impoverished women and they could help us with our theoretical competence, through their command and critique of Scripture and the tradition.

*You fought to save ITER from being closed by Vatican order under Recife's new bishop. What do you think is behind this kind of intervention?*

My view is limited by this world I live in, but my impression is that the conflict opened by the Vatican is, without a doubt, a return to a vision of the church dominating the world. It's not a Conciliar vision of the church open to the world, but one of domination. Since the church isn't able to dialogue, it dominates by force—closing in on the people and the intellectuals, like any other dictatorial regime.

Many intellectuals, men and women, can't secure tenure at institutions. Not just theologians, but many people—economists, sociologists, psychologists—are co-opted into making an alliance with the conservative church.

I believe the center of the problem is a vision of the world, of humanity and of the role of the church. I think that the institutional church, not the church as people of God, but the hierarchical church is afraid of the world. This is the typical behavior of someone who's afraid—the fearful one attacks, protects herself or himself, uses prisons for those who think differently. The fearful one does not dialogue.

It's interesting that peasants and many women at the base don't even bother with all this! They go on with life! Other things interest them—survival, bread, food. As the people say, this is *briga do branco* [literally, "fight of the white"], which means "This doesn't interest me." *Briga do branco.*

*You came from a middle-class, educated background and chose to live among the poor. Do you see other people from your class making similar choices?*

I have the impression that most people from the rich or middle-classes feel sorry for the poor, but this sorry doesn't go very far. Ultimately, people want to save their own skin and have their place in the sun.

I'm convinced of the terribly urgent necessity for the rich and middle-class to open up to a more human dimension of their own riches, which, most times, are made from the direct or indirect exploitation of the poor. To discover the human meaning of wealth is to discover a happiness, a well-being, a meaning for that which is the fruit of human hands, that every person has a right to.

The wealth of the rich is inhuman because it rests on the death of others. So we need a movement of collective consciousness to change the rules of the economic game, the political game, the ideological game. If the rich keep guarding their own interests, then, without a doubt, they'll be the first ones responsible for the destruction of human life and all life on the face of the earth.

*Have you found feminism to be a point of contact between the poor and non-poor?*

There's a problem here. To the extent that feminist groups make an option for a new world or egalitarian values, yes. But I've seen groups that understand feminism as penetrating the world of business and industry while maintaining the structure of society as it is. In this kind of feminism, there's no possibility of dialogue. For example, I attended a women's meeting in Montreal on the issue of power, but the great majority had such an elitist perspective of feminism!

There are feminists, however, who want a new political, economic, social and religious order. A dialogue is possible with a feminism that is committed to the poor.

*What message do you want to send to people in the First World?*

You in the First World need a more critical stance before the political choices of your governments. We all must be united under values that preserve human life and dignity, that establish justice in our relations.

I think a revolution is possible. I'm not talking about taking up arms, but the revolution of people who are beginning to build from little things, obeying the values deep within themselves that will save humanity and the earth.

I'd like to see us make an alliance of people that want to save the earth through values such as respecting the human person, man and woman. An alliance of life.

I'd like us to join hands—not as we in the Third World needing the money and wisdom of the First World, but as we human beings, women and men, wanting to create a new face of humanity, a new and different world!

# 15

# José Maria Pires

My commitment to the poor is an outcome of the Gospel.

It's not an ideological proposal, but a theological one born of faith. It's a hope for a new world, that great mountain with food for everyone!

This hope animates my commitment as a bishop to the cause of the poor—not almsgiving, but encouraging the poor to organize themselves and to be the subjects of social transformation.

*José Maria Pires, known to the people as "Dom José," was the first black bishop in Brazil, a country second only to Nigeria in black population. Born to a farming family in the countryside of Minas Gerais, the young José Maria became a parish priest, then director of a high school and then a bishop. For the past twenty-five years, he has served in João Pessoa, Paraíba, in Brazil's drought- and poverty-stricken Northeast. Dom José, as he is known today, has long been a voice demanding justice for farmers and advocating nonviolent means of social change.*

*When I first wrote to Dom José requesting an interview, he kindly responded that he would be available on return from the Northeastern bishops' ad limina visit to Rome—the periodic visit required of all bishops. During our interview, the bishop chose not to say much about the visit or the tensions between the Vatican and the Brazilian church, but another bishop in Brazil's northeast confided to me that it was truly a depressing visit. The Brazilian bishops were treated like children and lectured at rather than listened to. Nor did anyone in the Roman Curia—after twelve days*

Bishop José Maria Pires admires the trees in his back yard garden.

*and four visits with the Pope—mention the twenty-five year an-*
*niversary of Vatican II (their* ad limina *visit was in 1990).*

*Dom José brought me to a corner of his household's kitchen*
*for our interview, where our conversation was accompanied by*
*the cacophony of clanging pots, screeching kettles and ringing*
*phones. After our interview he proudly showed me his lush back*
*yard, complete with productive beehives and a small shack shel-*
*tering a huge drum of honey.*

*When I told Dom José that he looks a little bit like Nelson Man-*
*dela, he beamed, "We're even the same age—seventy-one!"*

જ્ર જ્ર જ્ર

I was born in the countryside. My father was a farmer.

As a child, I worked the fields and grew to love the land
deeply. That's why I have a little piece of land today. We grow let-
tuce and cabbage and raise bees. Yesterday I gathered twenty-
four liters of honey!

I wanted to be a priest since I was seven years old.

You see, conversion is very easy in the life of a peasant. The
farmer is a person of faith. He's not a prisoner to a schedule,
a sign-in sheet or a boss. This allows him to be a contemplative
of nature.

The farmer, he sees birth, growth, harvesting. This gives him
an idea of God as our friend and parent. He's a born contemplative because he lives so much closer to nature than people in
the city.

In the city, people are always rushing. Rushing to compete,
to produce, to be efficient. This may promote "progress," but if
you're not careful, it robs your humanity because you have to
run, run, run. It robs you of time to contemplate—to stop, pay
attention to a flower.

જ્ર જ્ર જ્ર

My conversion to the poor was more gradual.

> This *favela* is typical of João Pessao, the city where
> Dom José lives and works. Of all the Brazilian
> bishops, he is at the forefront of defending the
> rights of the street children, prostitutes, the land-
> less and rural workers.

As a pastor, only twenty years old, I occasionally defended the poor who were cheated by the large landowners. The rich landowners began calling me a communist!

My commitment to the poor is an outcome of the Gospel. It's not an ideological proposal, but a theological one born of faith. It's a hope for a new world, that great mountain with food for everyone!

This hope animates my commitment as a bishop to the cause of the poor—not almsgiving, but encouraging the poor to organize themselves and to be the subjects of social transformation.

You see, the Brazilian church has lived a unique situation— a situation that has obligated us to take up a stance in defense of the poor and human rights, and perhaps we can help others do the same.

As a young bishop, I participated in Vatican II.

Unlike the other bishop conferences at Vatican II, we had the joy of staying in the same house together, all eighty-five bishops from Brazil! So, almost every afternoon, we'd gather together— discussing, debating and listening to the views of Catholic, Protestant and Orthodox theologians.

The unity which came from sharing the same quarters was very evident after the Council.

Returning from the Council, we began to meet and ask, "Who is this 'People of God' that the Council spoke of?" And we saw that the People of God are the eighty percent of our population who are poor, those in our churches, who are so open to the Gospel. So the Church has to commit itself to the poor, because they are the ones who help organize the reign of God.

Vatican II showed us a church opened to the world, and, like I said, ours is a world of the poor. So we took up a very strong preferential option for the poor.

Because of this option, the bishops felt the need to simplify their own lives. Some left their residential palaces, lessened their daily demands and tried to foster a simpler lifestyle among the priests.

Simplicity of life can be a sign to others.

✞ ✞ ✞

In addition to Vatican II, the military dictatorship, which began in 1964, also forced us bishops to combat injustice, torture and other atrocities. As a block, we struggled to defend human rights.

We would visit political prisoners and go to the government to demand better conditions. We opened our churches as free spaces for those who needed it. We were often silenced, yet we continued struggling.

I don't know of any other episcopacy in the world that had such an opportunity to defend human rights—a testimony which comes from the Gospel. This wasn't because of our virtues, but because of the forces at work in our society and church.

ళ ళ ళ

For a long while, I was the only black bishop in Brazil.

When I was a young bishop, Pelé was a famous soccer star. Being the only black bishop at the time, the other bishops began calling me "Dom Pelé." But since then, Pelé has shown himself to be not very committed to the cause of blacks, so the bishops found the name didn't fit any more.

They began to call me "Dom Zumbi" after Zumbi dos Palmares, who struggled for the liberation of black slaves in Brazil.[†] This is much more meaningful!

I didn't wake up to black consciousness until 1978.

We were preparing for the Latin American Bishops meeting in Puebla. A group of young black people in São Paulo wrote me a long letter, saying what they hoped for from a black among the bishops. They shared the story of how the church in Brazil always looked down on blacks and their cause. Hence, blacks have no reason to rejoice over a church meeting. But since a black bishop was going to participate, they wanted to share their concerns and ideas.

---

[†]Zumbi dos Palmares lived during the seventeenth century in colonial Brazil. Since the beginning of that century, run-away slaves were organizing themselves in free democratic communities called *quilombos*. Zumbi was elected the leader of the most important *Quilombo dos Palmares*, a *quilombo* that also welcomed Indigenous persons and poor whites who were dissatisfied with the current colonial system. Zumbi, born in freedom in *Palmares*, was kidnapped and given as a "gift" to a Jesuit priest, who educated him in Latin, Greek and the classics. As an adult, Zumbi chose to return to *Palmares* to help lead the *quilombo* slave liberation movement. The government sent armies against *Palmares* and after many battles, Zumbi was finally killed on the 20th of November, 1695. The 20th of November is now "black consciousness day" in Brazil.

The end of the letter silenced me profoundly: "As a black person, you are our brother. As a bishop, you are our adversary."

From then on, I felt I had to be a brother, not just as a black person, but also as a bishop. A brother. To be a brother, I had to face myself and carry myself as a black person. I had to take up the cause of blacks, which I have done ever since.

This situation of blacks here is conditioned by the past.

Blacks came to Brazil as slaves and remained slaves for centuries. The master-slave relationship no longer exists, but the prejudice does. Whites feel superior before blacks, and blacks often feel inferior before whites.

This prejudice dominates social relations and is profoundly reflected in the Church. The statutes of religious congregations prohibited them from receiving black women, and seminaries made it tough for black men to enter!

So it's still hard to find black priests, bishops, diplomats or blacks in other leadership posts. Blacks are practically excluded—unless they are a great soccer player or performing artist. Common black people are marginalized.

*At least* forty percent of our population is of African descent! And the great majority of Catholics are black—but we only have seven black bishops, while you in the U.S. have thirteen, with a much smaller black population.

✠ ✠ ✠

Our struggle in Brazil first and foremost is against institutionalized violence—the complete organization of society against the poor.

Institutionalized violence gives rise to other violence—assaults, kidnappings, etc. We have to struggle against all violence, not just the consequences, but the institutionalized violence. We must struggle for a more just society.

We must take up arms in this struggle, but not conventional arms. We don't conquer violence with violence.

Unity among the poor is much more effective than all the weapons that powerful people have. All the big people need the small people! The small people create the stability of the big people. To the extent that the small people organize themselves, they are strong.

Imagine if in a city like João Pessoa all the cooks stopped cooking for others. Imagine if all the child care workers stopped watching the children. The big people can't move without the small ones! They need drivers, washers, housekeepers, etc.

So, as the poor become aware that their unity is a great strength, they can truly change society without using conventional arms.

Nonviolence isn't sitting back with your arms folded.

It is first recognizing that the very person who is your oppressor is also your brother or sister. One day he or she may stop being your oppressor, but they'll never stop being your brother or sister! So, I can't just do away with that person.

I want the person oppressing me to become reasonable. To do this, we must unite to show him or her that we're a force to be reckoned with. From there, they can be moved inside and become reasonable.

I call this "the pressure from margin to center." That is, the poor actually convert the rich to the extent that the poor organize themselves. They bring the rich to stop practicing injustice.

For example, if two or three hundred farm workers organize themselves and go to a large landowner and demand that he allow them to work some of his land, those workers are converting the person who was pressured! He gives in because of the pressure, but he ends up reflecting, "These people also have the right to live!"

The organization of the poor is a great strength.

So, *yes* to nonviolence, *no* to pacifism.

We need a struggle, but not a struggle armed with violence.

ﷺ ﷺ ﷺ

I think the biggest religious problem in Brazil is television. TV is helping "de-Christianize" Brazil.

It used to be that families at least met together for prayer, but now they don't meet at all! There are soap operas at six, at seven, then the news, then more soap operas. People are all in the same house, but they don't visit with one another. Time that was given to prayer is absorbed by the soap operas!

The content of family life is disappearing. People don't converse anymore. They don't discuss or fight *or* say nice things because they're all turned towards the TV!

I don't doubt that TV is a great instrument of communication. But it's become an instrument of *non*-communication for us. Religiously, I think this is a far more serious problem than the growth of Pentecostal sects.

☙ ☙ ☙

I believe in a God that wants a different and better world.

This faith sustains me in my life and struggles—believing in the One God sent, Jesus Christ, who gave his life for this cause, who rose and guaranteed victory for us. Not necessarily here and now, but victory *is* guaranteed.

I also have faith in the poor people who are on the journey.

If we had faith but never saw results, that would be very dry and rough. But then we feel that the people are responding—not to our appeals or incentives, but to a God who speaks to their hearts. The people are learning more and more to read the word of God in history and in the intimate reaches of themselves.

This nourishes my faith!

☙ ☙ ☙

*You have experienced how blacks are a minority in church leadership. What about women? How would you like to see the church change in regard to women?*

I have great hope for women because of the base communities where women are not marginalized or excluded. In the CEBs, women have the same opportunities as men and, because of their numbers, they're generally the community leaders. Around here they are also extraordinary ministers of baptism, holy communion and marriage to help when a pastor is absent!

Black women are marginalized by whites, but not by blacks. Black women have a very prominent position in black culture. She directs almost all of the religious celebrations. In the Afro-Brazilian religions, it's the women who participate in the sacred

Underneath the bust of Afro-Brazilian hero Zumbi, the plaque reads: Zumbi dos Palmares. Inaugurated November 20, 1988. "First cry of liberation in America and symbol of resistance by the black race." A victory of the Afro-cultural group *Ojuoba Axé Pioneiro*, on the centenary of the abolition of slavery in Brazil. Supported by the municipal office of Duque de Caxias. 1888/1988

banquet, eating first, then distributing to the participants.[††] Women should have the prominent position in society that she has in religious life.

I don't think the ordination of women is the most important thing. The most important thing is that women are recognized as equal to men. From there, the question of exercising the same religious functions as men will evolve with time. We can't yet predict how this will evolve.

But, the most important thing is the absolute need for the Church to break with machismo in order to give women the place to which they have a right.

*Must those who are born into privilege also break with their social class to give the poor a more equal place?*

The rich person has to pass by the road of the poor person. This doesn't mean becoming poor, but taking up the causes the poor struggle for—social change, a more just society. The poor aren't struggling to overthrow people, kill people, lord over them. They want a just society where everyone has what is necessary to live.

To the extent that a rich person enters this cause, which is the Gospel cause, he or she will be saved—through the poor. Christ announced truth for all people, but he announced it from the social place of the poor. So, we must walk by this road.

*Is it possible to create a liberation theology for or from the First World?*

I think that all theology should be liberation theology, because pressures and oppression exists on all sides, of all stripes.

But, if we generalize like this, the person who is poor from lack of food and money will be dropped to the second or third level of concern. For us in Latin America, liberation theology will reflect about the journey of this poor person who is eighty

---

[††]The Afro-Brazilian religion of Candomblé, which follows the tradition of the *orixás*, the ancestors, who animate the community of faith, gives men and women equal status. Often the community minister is a woman, known as the *mãe de santo*, literally, the "mother of the saint."

percent of the population who doesn't have what's necessary to survive.

But, in Europe and probably in the U.S. as well, I feel that overabundance can lead to dissatisfaction and even drug abuse. When one has "everything," a certain satiation actually creates discontent.

Also, the very fact of having everything makes us feel like we don't need others. So social relationships aren't relationships of my helping the other, but seeing how much another can serve my ends. I don't open myself to the other because I can survive without them! People like this become slaves to selfishness.

How can theology in the U.S. and Europe be a liberation theology? How can the Gospel really be lived where it is being forgotten? This reflection would be different from ours, because we're starting from the reality of the poor person without food, without land to work, with no school to study in, with no place in society or in the church. For you the starting point is how to become liberated from selfishness.

*Acts of solidarity would be a step beyond selfishness. What concrete things can people in the First World do to be in solidarity with the people of Brazil?*

First of all, both the U.S. and Europe should recognize that they are oppressing us. As the poet Eduardo Galeano says, they're opening our veins and taking our blood from our forests, from our land. It's a tremendous exploitation to take our raw materials and pay us a pittance, or lend us money to make things that will assist European or North American firms.

The second gesture of solidarity would be a greater interchange between us. A great value among Latin Americans is our hospitality, our capacity to welcome everyone—a very biblical value! We want to make friends—not just find people to donate something to us! We want to get to know you as a brother or sister. In our mutual efforts at getting to know each other, we show our solidarity.

Third, you can support the causes of the poor. The media can have this power to communicate, to show news in all corners of the world. The cause of the poor can be victorious much sooner if our sisters and brothers in Europe and the U.S. continue to campaign in favor of the poor of the Third World!

# 16

## Pedro Casaldáliga

Clearly, I'm not glorifying oppression, persecution or death. I don't just insist on the resurrection, I'm obsessed by the resurrection!

I say over and over again to our people—in celebrations and pastoral visits—that the single most Christian word we can pronounce is Easter.

I once wrote a poem that says,

*"This is our alternative:*
*live or resurrected, never dead!"*

Nominated by the bishops of Spain for the 1991 Nobel Peace Prize, Pedro Casaldáliga is himself bishop of São Felix do Araguaia, a remote diocese in the state of Mato Grosso, Brazil. Born in Catalonia, Spain, Dom Pedro is a Claretian missionary who has lived in Brazil since 1968. Internationally recognized for his commitment to nonviolence and his uncompromising defense of the poor and oppressed, Dom Pedro is also a poet whose verse has been read in many lands and languages.

I interviewed Dom Pedro at his simple home of clay and brick with cement floors. The diminutive priest wears plastic thongs, as do millions of Brazilians. For two days I observed his morning rituals: prayer in solitude at dawn, international news on his shortwave radio, prayer with his community, a simple breakfast of bread and coffee. His humility was evident in his every act—serving me lunch, clearing the dishes, typing away on a manual typewriter and instantly stopping his work when a neighbor appeared at the door to visit.

Dom Pedro invited me to stay the night, since São Felix do Araguaia is a long journey from any major city. He was just

231

*recovering from pneumonia, so we talked a bit one afternoon and continued the next morning. Visiting in the garden behind his home, a kitten played at our feet and a humming bird occasionally flitted by. Ever the poet, Dom Pedro marveled at each creature with attentive delight.*

ᔥ ᔥ ᔥ

I am from Catalonia, Spain, in the province of Barcelona, which is between the sea and the mountains. I'm sixty-two years—an old horse! I'm the child of a cow wrangler, a simple, humble family with peasant roots.

I'm more or less a poet. And, I'm now Latin American by passion!

ᔥ ᔥ ᔥ

My spiritual conversion happened quite early. I don't know if you believe in the Holy Spirit working in children. I do!

When I was eight, my mother's thirty-three year old brother, Luís, was assassinated by the anarchists during the Spanish revolution. I helped hide some religious people who might have been put in concentration camps or murdered. Later, I helped some clandestine priests with the Mass during the war.

So, my adolescence was marked by a certain heroism.

When I was eleven, I entered the diocesan seminary and later joined the Claretian Missionaries. My option was always for the missions. I had a bit of the mentality of helping the "poor little black people and Indians." However, my superiors gave me other responsibilities. Then, at our congregation's 1967 general chapter to implement Vatican II, I gave the ultimatum: "I'm going." That's how I got to Brazil.

I am actually the first priest to really live and stay in this town!

By now, our pastoral work has evolved to include liturgical celebrations, sacraments, catechesis, the pastoral health project, education, the pastoral projects to demand human rights and justice, which means denouncing the violence and defending the peasants' and Indians' right to land.

ᔥ ᔥ ᔥ

When I first arrived in Latin America in 1968, there was a full military dictatorship in Brazil.

Originally, the church hierarchy supported the dictatorship because of its fear of communism. But when the abuses and domination grew, they adopted a more prophetic and critical attitude.

The Brazilian Bishops Conference (CNBB) nearly unanimously voted on documents promoting social justice, land reform, education and the rights of the Indigenous. This was unique! Even today, the three countries with the most religious persons murdered are El Salvador, Haiti and Brazil.

The 1970s were a revolutionary decade of Latin American consciousness—even ecclesiastically, given Medellín in 1968. All of this gave us a greater awareness and inspired us to take up the option for the poor.

Also, the region where I work was and is violent. It's a region of Indigenous, peasants and large landowners. Many have been murdered in the conflict between landowners and peasants—without names, without coffins. We buried many people.

Really, in this situation, there was no way to take another option. And we have suffered because of our option for the poor.

My friend, Father João Bosco Burnier, was shot while standing next to me. Many friends have been killed, and, yes, I've received death threats for years. The landowners form their own death squads to threaten those who challenge them.

� ᛜ ᛜ

My faith sustains me in these trying times. And the fact of being a bishop gives me a specific responsibility. We're obliged to become what our friends call us to be.

I thank God that I've never had a great faith crisis! My writing helps. Communicating in an open way about your life experiences naturally brings one to a certain coherence. And I think poetry, a love of nature and a childlike sensitivity all help me to live with more naturalness and vibrancy, overcoming problems.

They say a poet is born, so I guess I was born a poet!

This means I always carry with me a type of vibrancy before everything—a humming bird, a kitten, the face of a child, the stars, a death, loneliness, despair, God.

This *pulses* in me.

In one of my poems I say that no one can accompany me to-tally. I've heard that you can measure someone's personality by their capacity for solitude.

Ultimately, we're all alone. I alone have to answer for myself before society and God, because we aren't a collectivized mass, we're individual persons in communion. This is the greatness and tragedy of being human.

Now, this solitude can be filled with silence, contemplation and personal growth. But it can also be anguished or morbid. For one who has faith, who lives serving others, who loves nature, solitude is never morbid.

ॐ ॐ ॐ

I thank God, who's accompanied me with pretty clear signs. The martyrdom I lived as a child and have lived so intensely here in Latin American has been for me a great sacrament.

When you live so close to death, including the death of mar-tyrdom, is seems that you are always on the ultimate frontier. That is, life cannot be banal because you are so close to suffer-ing; at times close to despair, but also close to heroism.

But how do we value martyrdom without glorifying human suffering?

How to value the cross. . . . This is the same question, isn't it?

We know that the cross is cursed when it's not a redemptive cross. We venerate, glorify, perhaps long for martyrdom not as death, but as a witness. Not as losing life, but as giving life. Je-sus said this is the greatest love.

The familial and historic environment of my whole life, from infancy to religious formation to Latin America, has made martyrdom something natural in my life. I also believe, like the Italians, that "a beautiful death beautifies all of life." This stimulation to generosity and radical giving helps one to over-come the monotonies of life.

Clearly, I'm not glorifying oppression, persecution or death. I don't just insist on the resurrection, I'm obsessed by the resur-rection!

I say over and over again to our people—in celebrations and pastoral visits—that the single most Christian word we can pro-nounce is Easter. I once wrote a poem that says, "This is our al-ternative: live or resurrected, never dead!"

ఌ ఌ ఌ

The contemplative life isn't just important—it's my whole life!
I always say, the more radically we are revolutionaries, the more
radically we should be contemplatives.

And what is prayer? Prayer is a personal and collective celebration of faith.

Thank God that in our church of liberation we continually
give more celebration to faith! Our prayer—alone, in teams, the
pilgrimages for land, the huge meetings of the CEBs, remember-
ing the martyrs—they're all celebrative!

We bring celebration to the struggle. Latin America—concretely, the Indigenous, black and the feminine world—is water,
forest, birds, dance, music. The churches want to incarnate
themselves in these expressions.

We often associate "struggle" with "armed struggle."

In Latin America, "struggle" has a very broad and varied
meaning. It is a combative spirit, but it can also be our daily
work, commitment and engagement.

Clearly, I'm not in favor of violence. First and foremost in this
world, we should destroy the arms factories once and for all. If
the bishops and pastors and presidents and politicians of the
world were sufficiently honest and courageous, we would kneel
in front of every single arms factory to prevent their continued
production!

Now it's easy for the empire, for capitalism, for the dictators to
condemn *only* the struggle of the poor and to forget about the root
of all violence—the institutionalized violence of the very empire.

ఌ ఌ ఌ

In my twenty years here, I've sought to work in teams with
religious and laity, married or single. We make this option to mu-
tually complement one another. We pray and eat together, but
also have personal space to cultivate our particular identities.

We try to live close to the people, so you won't find us in
palaces or curias.

If I lived alone as a bishop in a palace, with a secretary and
a cook, I wouldn't have the opportunity to live the daily problems
of the people! I wouldn't have the chance to hear the women
neighbors who come here to talk with Sister Irene about health
problems, or with Maria, the lawyer, about land problems.

Some people are surprised to see that I live like this! I think that mixed living conditions open our horizons. It helps us walk with our feet on the ground.

As a bishop, I recognize that we, the hierarchy, are the main ones responsible for the evil that occurs, and for the good that doesn't occur, in the church. I heard a joke that there can only be bishops in hell—others don't stand a chance of getting in!

At a national meeting of the CEBs, I invited the bishops to kneel in front of the people in repentance. So often we did not have the prophetic courage to denounce or announce. Many times the Christian people, especially women and the poor, haven't had the opportunity to participate. It's no doubt because the hierarchy closed itself to dialogue.

Hence, the *mea culpa* should begin with the cupola [the dome or top of a structure, referring to the church hierarchy].

ᛰᛰᛰ

I always say, God will take care of us after we're dead—we have to take care of now until death! Chapter 25 of Matthew puts it clearly: hunger, thirst, imprisonment will judge us. A faith that isn't expressed in works is dead.

And our works can't be just individual, they must address structures as well. Still, I always say that the biggest problem God will ever have is to condemn someone.

God is love, as St. John says, and love doesn't like to condemn. God sent us his Son not to judge, but to save us.

If I could save any one biblical text, I'd choose this: "God so loved the world that God sent God's only Son, not to judge the world, but to save it."

ᛰᛰᛰ

*You don't claim to be a theologian, yet you have often spoken out in defense of liberation theology. What does liberation theology mean to you?*

First we must acknowledge that liberation theology was born more from the journeying feet of the Latin American Christian people than from the thinking heads of theologians! These communities of people who are oppressed and believers, collective martyrs, gave rise to this theology.

This is a Christian theology situated in space and time. It denounces structural and personal sin and announces the good news, not only for those beyond death, but for those who are still living.

Many times when I'm giving the host during communion I say, "This is the Lamb of God who takes away the sin, slavery and death of the world." The Bible tells us that our ultimate enemy, death, will be overcome. But there are many other penultimate enemies! Hunger, sickness, oppression, marginalization, sin in general. These are our enemies that also have to be overcome.

*Five centuries ago the Church converted many Indians by force. As a neighbor to these communities, do you think the Indigenous make a unique contribution to Christianity?*

Yes! Some anthropologists from Europe thought that the Indigenous of Latin America didn't have religion. Then they discovered that for the Indigenous, everything was religion! I wrote a song for an Indian liturgy, "Our dance is worship, our life is worship, our death is worship!"

Also, they bring this dimension of a contemplative life—this profound, spontaneous communion with nature, this capacity for hours of silence in the forest, the naturalness with which they converse with the transcendent, their multiplicity of myths, symbols. We sometimes rationalize our lives so much that we become parched and cold. We should re-cultivate a spirituality of silence, myth, a living sense of God and neighbor here and beyond death!

*Do you think that ecology can be a point of solidarity between the First and Third Worlds?*

I'd say this: I can only defend ecology if, above and beyond all else, I understand that the maximum ecology is the human being. The most important thing isn't the house, but the one who dwells in the house, and the universe is our home.

So, if ecology is only a bucolic sentimentalism, if it's only a fear that we can't get good quality lumber or that pollution will reach us, if it doesn't value the Indigenous people and the people of the Third World, then it's selfish and colonialist.

It's also important for you to see that you in the First World are sending us the pollution you don't want—chemical factories, nuclear waste, even medical experiments too risky for the U.S. The invasion of American TV is also a pollution!

Ecology can be a point of solidarity only if it's understood as the defense and respect of the global condition of our singular, interdependent universe.

*Living in community with women must make you sensitive to women's struggle for equality in the church. Do you think men fear the liberation of women?*

I have no doubt that men must lose privilege for women to have equality. All of us—myself or any of us—who are accustomed to another theology, practice or relationships, we need a *conversion.* But ultimately, there's no biblical or theological argument preventing the equal presence of women in all church ministries. I don't see anything improper about a woman becoming a bishop or pope!

*I read the letter you wrote about your visit to Rome. Can you describe the problems you've had with the Vatican?*

I didn't do my *ad limina* visit because I felt that it didn't foster a dialogue. It ended up being very formal, a big expense of time and money, and many bishops felt they were being treated like children. They hardly had six or seven minutes to talk to the Pope!

I finally wrote a letter to the Pope saying that I'd go there with pleasure if he felt it opportune. Ultimately, I think the visit was worth it, and the Pope recognized that the new way of doing the *ad limina* visit proposed by the Brazilian bishops could be good for other bishops' conferences.

*What do you think is at the heart of these kinds of tensions?*

I think that the root is ethnocentricity. Rome is a unicultural center. I believe in the ministry of Peter, which is indispensable for unity, but it should be more open and flexible. The Catholic church lacks catholicity! Until now, we've had a Western, European church, which impedes true Catholic inculturation. To be faithful we should be incarnate in every time, place, culture and history!

I also think there's a certain fear—a lack of trust in the Spirit. We confuse unity with uniformity. The Spirit blows where it will! Pentecost was a multicultural phenomenon, windows and doors open and all languages spoken! I don't know why we don't trust that the Spirit will incarnate the church in any culture or language.

*You have made a clear choice to live like the people you serve. For others, how might a non-poor person live out the option for the poor?*

Look, I myself, by the very fact of being a bishop, am not poor. Anyone who goes through a university or seminary or novitiate isn't poor, because we have more possibilities, a culture, a backing that simple poor people lack.

But I, or any relatively bourgeois intellectual or family, can and should "betray" our class and opt for the causes of the poor—the organizations, demands and movements of the poor who are trying to liberate themselves. You as a journalist can work for the International Monetary Fund, but instead you're trying to serve the Third World and the church of the poor, in solidarity.

*Does this mean we must renounce our privilege or put it at the service of the poor?*

I'm not going to ask that First World families go hungry, but they can renounce certain privileges. We should simplify. For example, we get a lot of help from European groups who create a "self-tax," tithing part of their salary to help the Third World. They renounce trips, luxuries, foods. Solidarity isn't throwing a party to raise alms twice a year! The rich person shouldn't merely be giving alms, but should truly have mercy and compassion on others, as Jesus himself did.

When I begin to understand that every other person, every poor person is an equal to myself, I can no longer retain my privileges, because to do so would be robbery. I cannot merely give donations, I must pay back what I owe. There's a difference.

*Do you think that rich people also suffer a certain kind of poverty,*
*from consumerism or a life of abundance?*

I'm convinced that consumerism, by definition, consumes
humanity. It consumes freedom of spirit and creates insatiable
appetites. If you have two, you want three; if you have three, you
want four! We end up being well-fed, but empty within.

Also, consumerism kills cultural identities, creating uniformity. You can get the same cereals, shoes and music in the whole
world! We're losing the ethnic and cultural richness of individual
cultures. We end up becoming a uniformized humanity, which is
the opposite of a unified humanity.

We're even endangering the health of our organisms and the
health of our universe! But I believe that no one, by nature, kills
him or herself. Humanity as humanity doesn't commit suicide.
So I believe that humanity will begin to open its eyes, and return
to a naturalness and a certain sobriety.

You know, when you have everything, you value nothing. I've
seen people with ten brands of cheese in their refrigerators. Their
biggest problem is choosing what kind of cheese they want! How
many times I traveled by horseback in the backlands and arrived
at the house of a peasant—and the only thing they could give
me was a *little* cup of water! But, that cup of water is so valuable!
So welcomed!

We need a civilization of love and sharing, a certain sobriety
that will be a model for our children. Nature teaches us this. You
see children of rich people who have lots of expensive, new toys
in their house, and yet they get a stick, some twine and a tin can
and make a horse! And all the toys that daddy bought just sit
there!

I think that sobriety makes us truly free and happy.


*So we also need liberation from our excesses?*

We need re-education for a certain sobriety and spiritual harmony, to respect our bodies, respect nature, respect others. Look
how easily people kill or commit suicide. How easily people di-
vorce. How easily people abort. How easily people sell arms. Arms
factories are the most lucrative business in the world today!

I believe the poor person can offer the rich a certain liberation, because there's a liberty of spirit which poverty facilitates—
the capacity to share, basic values, enthusiasm. When U.S.

citizens or Europeans come to the Third World, they feel a certain liberty, sharing and simplicity here—a spontaneous joy that they don't usually feel. Maybe you all have "everything" but are still lacking a certain "something."

The poor person should constantly be a sacrament for the rich person. God enters all sacraments, but the most universal sacrament God chooses is the poor. Even the person without Christian faith will be saved to the degree that he or she welcomes the sacrament of the poor person, their sister or brother in need.

*For years you have been taking "solidarity trips" to Central America. What kind of solidarity would you like from First World peoples?*

Remember that I'm also from the First World!

First, people should open their eyes to see structural sin, which is the very existence of a First and Third World. As long as there's a First World, there won't be peace because there won't be justice or sharing. We should do away with both First and Third Worlds! We have created this situation, so we can also do away with it.

Secondly, since official organisms, like governments, the World Bank and multinational corporations, have no interest in changing this situation, we need non-official organisms in the First World—ecclesial communities, youth groups, intellectuals—with a sense of solidarity and social consciousness to break with this system of oppression. There are so many ways—interchanges, financial help, civil disobedience at arms factories.

*Do you have much hope for this liberation from First and Third Worlds?*

This is how I see it: We in Latin American have had revolutions, we've spilled our blood against the empires and the military dictatorships. Now it's time to have a revolution against pseudo-democracy. I was listening to President Bush on the radio this morning, speaking of the "market economy and private property"—that is, neo-liberal capitalism, which is a pseudo-democracy, a democracy merely in votes. This isn't political or economic or social or ethnic-cultural democracy.

One also feels throughout the world a return to conservatism in the church. The nominations of bishops, control of bishops' conferences, closing seminaries, the censoring of liberation theologians, and especially the criticism of the popular reading of the Bible. This brings many people to discouragement. But I have hope.

I have hope because I believe that history doesn't repeat itself. History moves forward! Certain things are irreversible—the new awareness and freedom inside the church that didn't exist before, the participation of lay persons in the church, the CEBs, the new theologies, the new ways of reading the Bible, ecumenism at the base. Above all that, in the more marginalized sectors of the church, so much martyrdom is flowering, so much testimony spilled in blood. This is irreversible!

*Do you have any special message for people in the U.S.?*

Yes, help us do away with the empire of capitalism, militarism, consumerism, colonialism, privilege. Get to know other worlds and have an appreciation for friendly equality among peoples and cultures. The U.S. is not "more" than Haiti or Guatemala or El Salvador! We are all human beings—one people should be equal to another people in possibilities, in dignity, in liberty!

Help us by protesting the hypocrisy within the U.S.—all the U.S. interventions in the world, "saving" the world with its predatory politics which violate human rights in El Salvador and all over the Third World. As a multicultural and multi-ethnic people, and with a great legal tradition of freedom, you have yet to live out this multi-cultural freedom in an authentic, human, fraternal way. I hope that we can soon invert the Monroe doctrine: America for all Americans, not only for the Americans of the U.S.!

In the United States there is always a Trojan horse of international solidarity, there in the heart of the empire! Many people from the United States are in Central America, El Salvador, Nicaragua—even giving their lives in martyrdom.

Yes, history moves forward.

# Afterword

## Robert McAfee Brown

What words abound here:
  freedom, liberation, structural violence
    but most of all   on every page   the gospel word of *life*
    heard most of all from those whose daily visitant is death
    who start their days without a crust of bread
    their only hope that someone else will notice and provide
They want to change all that
    breaking the chains of exploitation
    forged by oligarchs and bankers
    so that power is not exclusive to the privileged
    but a privilege and right for all who live and breathe
    and love
The church sustains them all, despite its inner contradictions
    Occasionally a bishop lives among his people
    spurning the palace set aside for him
    He blesses bread and wine upon God's Table
    and makes it part of his exalted role
    to fight for food for all the unexalted
    reminding those so nourished
    that every table is "God's Table"
    save those who have a compact with the rich
The women are the strong ones   finding untapped strength
    in broken bodies
        to stand against oppression
        to mobilize for justice
        to challenge unjust privilege
            (no longer hidden in the *status quo*
            but there for all to see)

and work for change in every part of life
No matter what their station
   sister    Sister    mother    teacher
they organize the masses in the name of God's own Son
through whom they are empowered
to nurture God's own daughters too
and anyone in need
How shall we sing of them?    Only by listening
   only by silence
   a silence   broken not a moment before
   we hear their cry to *us*
      work for justice
      share what you have
      join together
      knock on all doors
      watch
      pray
      organize
Be with us   sisters and brothers everywhere   they pray
      so that our cry can fill your hearts
      and together we can sing in choruses
      that will not cease until
      all God's folk are one (and all folk are God's folk)
      and forces of evil are constrained to goodness
      and there is no more crying
      and there is no more hunger
      and there is no more terror
      and the new heaven and the new earth are planted
   squarely in our midst

# "The People is Poet"

## By Maria da Silva Miguel

One day a woman cried, "I am a Warrior!"
and the echo of her voice was heard beyond the borders.
I am Woman-Mother and Warrior,
the stove is no longer my limit.
I am called queen of the home,
but I am greater than ocean and sea.
I am Mother, I give life,
I am a Woman, Pain.
I am a Warrior, a Bird—I sing!
I raise up my people and pull them out of slavery,
my name is Liberation!
Whoever wants to find me, I'm not only in the home,
I'm in the struggle, I'm a Warrior!
I am Black, I am Poor, I am Old and nearly Illitcrate,
Everyone knows me—
I am the remnant who dreams of happiness and love
I am merely Maria Miguel!

# Appendix I

*Dates of interviews:*

| | |
|---|---|
| Maria da Lourdes Silva Miguel | 9/22/90 |
| Maria Salomé Costa | 9/22/90 |
| Edilson da Herculano Silva | 9/25/90 |
| Maria Goreth do Nascimento Barradas | 9/08/90 |
| Antoinha Lima Barros | 9/07/90 |
| Lori Altmann | 10/15/90 |
| Frei Betto | 10/12/90 |
| Silvia Regina de Lima Silva | 10/03/90 |
| Clodovis Boff | 10/02/90 |
| Leonardo Boff | 10/01/90 |
| Carlos Mesters | 9/30/90 |
| Tereza Maria Pompéla Cavalcanti | 10/02/90 |
| Ivone Gebara | 10/10/90 |
| Rubem Alves | 9/18/90 |
| Bishop José Maria Pires | 10/09/90 |
| Bishop Pedro Casaldáliga | 10/26–27/90 |

# Appendix II

*Rio Maria Committee*
    c/o Madeleine Adriance
    238 Charles Street
    Cambridge, MA 02141–2004
    phone/fax: 617–868–4828
    e-mail: riomariausa@agc.org
Rio Maria, in the state of Pará, is one of the most violent areas of Brazil. Peasants and church workers are harassed, persecuted, and assassinated as they struggle for land reform. The Rio Maria Committee was organized in response to the request for foreign solidarity with these people who risk their lives in the struggle for justice. The Committee organizes urgent letter-writing campaigns.

*Amnesty International/ Brazil Urgent Action Program*
    P.O. Box 1270
    Nederland, CO 80466–1270
    phone: 303–440–0913 / fax: 303–258–7881
    telex: 454320 UAUSA

*BASE (Brazil Action & Solidarity Exchange)*
    c/o Global Exchange
    2141 Mission St. #202
    San Francisco, CA 94110
    phone: 415–255–7296
    e-mail: base@igc.apc.org
BASE is a group of Brazilians and non-Brazilians, primarily in the San Francisco Bay Area, working directly with human rights, environmental groups and other popular organizations throughout the Americas in solidarity with Brazil. The suggested $25.00 membership fee includes a subscription to the bi-lingual BASE newsletter, which includes information on Brazil that cannot be found anywhere else in print in the U.S.